Secret Art of the
Ninja

Secret Art of the
Ninja

PETER LEWIS

PRION

Published by Prion Books Ltd.,
32-34 Gordon House Road
London NW5 1LP

First published in 1988 by Ward Lock Ltd.,
Revised edition 1997
Copyright © Peter Lewis 1988, 1997

A catalogue record for this book is available from the
British Library

ISBN   1 85375 270 3

Cover design by Bob Eames
Printed and Bound in Great Britain by
Creative Print and Design, Wales

For Nigel, Paul, and Caroline Lewis
For without whom nothing has meaning

Contents

Introduction

He who overcomes others is strong
He who overcomes himself is mighty

ELITE fighting units have existed in practically every civilization since the dawn of time. The Romans had their Praetorian Guard, the ancient Greeks their army of Spartans. Throughout history specialist groups have been established for the sole purpose of their expertise in weaponry and waging war to win at any cost. Quite often these small groups were successful where huge armies were not. Highly trained personnel, honed to perfection through intensive specialist training, can and have wreaked havoc by infiltrating unseen behind enemy lines to ply their trade with devastating results. Even in the modern era of warfare, governments have initiated the forming of such elite brigades to tactically strike at the very heart of the enemy's bosom, and such groups as the US Delta Force and Great Britain's Special Air Service carry on the traditions of espionage and covert activities.

A special breed

In all of these specialist units, past and present, the common factor was that they were all a very special breed of men – men in peak physical condition, experts in their chosen field, and absolutely committed in their endeavours. But in each case, these men were recruited from an existing army and then selected for specialist training. In a few short months an intensive and gruelling training regimen produced a combat-ready soldier who, in terms of expertise, was far in advance of the ordinary infantryman. If one could take that intensive training a quantum leap forwards, and extend the few months into 18 years or so, the end product would probably be little short of a superman – a warrior whose mental and physical skills would be truly awesome. Such a unit does in fact exist, and its elite warrior traditions stretch back in time more than a thousand years. They are the ninja, the practitioners of the art of ninjutsu.

Introduction

Deadliest fighting machine

No fighting unit has captured the imagination in recent years more than Japan's legendary ninjas. The ninja has often been described as the deadliest fighting machine in the history of warfare. These black-garbed warriors swept through the pages of Japan's turbulent history leaving mayhem and death in their wake. Totally without morals, these assassins of the night killed without fear or favour, hiring themselves out to the highest bidder. Trained from birth, the ninja's only aim was completely to master techniques of espionage, weapons, unarmed combat, poisons and psychology. These skills were necessary in allowing the ninja to gather information through their clandestine activities and report to their superiors everything they had learned. The ninja and their black arts flourished for over 600 years – until the coming of modernization. Then the ninja clans, as they were known, disbanded. Some were lost for ever, but a few gained employment either with government agencies or on the other side of the law, in the pay of the Japanese criminal organizations known as 'Yakuza'. Thus in a perverted sense they kept alive the traditions and practices of the black assassins.

Introduction

The survival of the ninja

It does seem quite incredible that a whole society of people could live in a microcosm that devoted its every endeavour to killing, and that it could survive with this one theme at its core for so many centuries. It did, because circumstances allowed it to. Tremendous political upheavals were taking place at the time as a feudal Japan clawed its way up to form a civilized society and men of greed with a thirst for wealth and power saw opportunities to create empires for themselves. In doing so they created a market in which a skilled killer was, virtually unassailably, able to murder anyone at will. Such was the ninja's skill; in their deadly trade no one was safe from the assassin's dagger. From the ninja hierarchy right down to the field operator, they spread across medieval Japan like the tentacles of an octopus. It was an espionage organization of which the Western powers of the 20th century would have been envious.

The state serving the military

In his book *Vom Kriege* (On War) the 19th-century Prussian soldier and strategist Karl von Clausewitz stated that 'war is a continuation of politics by other means'. Napoleon taught that the universal currency of politics is power, and that power resides in the ability to wreak physical destruction. Clausewitz gave priority

Introduction

to civilian authority over the military. The military is supposed to serve the state, not vice versa. Napoleon thought along similar lines although he used the military to gain his own ends. But in Japan for nearly half a millennium the opposite occurred. The military ran the country in a warrior class dominated society. With the Emperor merely heading the regime as a puppet, the real power rested with at first the Bakufu, followed in later centuries by a Shogunate.

The rise of the ninja

For more than five centuries the country was in a virtual state of war, albeit internal and political. In that time great families or clans rose from obscurity to great power and fell into quite literal extinction, some almost overnight. Into this warrior society with its strict code of honour and the ethic of 'noblesse oblige' entered the ninja. They became the tool by which the warrior families sought to gain power. To a certain extent one could not have existed without the other. It wasn't until the country united under a central governing power in the 17th century and subsequently closed its doors to the outside world for another 200 years that the demise of the assassin clans finally came about. The history of Japan proper barely records the inestimable effect that the ninja clans had on the development of a unified government and its emergence into the modern world. Perhaps credence is not freely or justly given simply because the ninja and their trade of death by assassination are surreptitiously brushed under the carpet by the nation makers − in the hope that history forgets the black garbed Shadow Warriors.

A way of life

Some may argue that the ninja were not really an elite fighting group and that to classify them as such, alongside the more reputable elite units of the past, does a disservice to the latter. Not so. To look at the ninja clans merely as a people who traded in death is to miss the underlying theme of their existence. Espionage and murder were their stock in trade. The warlords of Japan for 600 years or more saw to it that they were never out of work. Yet if the strife and political expediency of the military government within Japan had not happened, the ninja, being deeply religious, would have developed along a different vein.

Many societies in our Western World have had secret societies, cult groups whose aim it was to undermine the political regime of the time. The sect of the *Nizari Ismaili Muslim*, better known as the Cult of the Assassins, was one such group. This dissident Shiite sect had formed a heresy within the Islamic

Introduction

faith and under their leader Rashid al Sinan (known as the old man of the mountains), waged war with fanatical zeal against the Christians (crusaders) and Muslims alike for well over 200 years. In fact the very name 'Assassin' comes from the arabic word 'hashshashin' meaning hashish eaters. (Hashish is a cannabis type drug.) Under the influence of hashish the followers of this sect would steal out into the night and kill whoever they had been hired to kill, very rarely failing in their missions.

The Sultans and Caliphs of the Middle East lived in fear and terror of these dagger-wielding extremists and surrounded themselves with whole armies of bodyguards. Later generations of assassin chiefs such as Hasan bin Sabbah wielded so much of the political power in Syria and Persia that it was usually better to agree with them rather than suffer the consequences.

The Cult of the Assassins perfected murder to a fine art and acted in the name of their religion and their chief. However, it wasn't so much a way of life for them as an enforced directive under the influence of mind-altering substances (hashish), with the offer of reaching a heavenly paradise upon completion of a mission. Almost all Assassins died in the execution of their mission. Therefore, although the ninja and the Assassins both worked towards the same ends, political powerplays being the prime motivators, the Assassins were a fanatical group while for the ninja it was a way of life. From the cradle to the grave, from father to son, clan to clan, they knew no other role than the niche carved by their ancestors.

The ninja live on

With the advent of the popular martial arts in the 1970s ninjutsu shed its cloak of past infamy and established itself as a respectable martial discipline. The popularity of ninjutsu took off at an astonishing rate worldwide. Spurred on by media promotions, such as TV, video and the movies, the Assassins' art emerged into the 1980s as a fighting art *par excellence*. An art whereby its adepts could train not only in unarmed combat and weaponry but also adopt principles of ninja philosophy as a guide for living life and facing day-to-day trials and tribulations with impunity.

Born of Blood –
Ninja History

Arouse a bee, and it will come at you with the force of a dragon

THE exact origins of the ninja and their art of nin-jutsu are shrouded in ancient myths. Legends abound as to their early beginnings, some believing they were the descendants of 'Tengu', the devil bird of Japanese mythology. Most historians now accept that ninjutsu was founded through political and religious upheaval aroung the end of the 6th century in Japan. However, although the first ninja clans established themselves in Japan, it is to China we must look for their origin.

Art of War

In China during the period known as the Warring States, around 500 BC, a great Chinese general and military strategist named Sun Tsu wrote a book on warfare called *Art of War*, which was a treatise on the exact science of subjects such as offensive strategy, weakness and strengths of the enemy, terrain, employment of spies, guerrilla warfare, and vulnerability. This book was regarded as standard reading for Chinese intellectuals and military men and even the Taoist and Buddhist priests were well acquainted with its contents. Sun Tsu was well aware that combat involved a great deal more than just a collision of armed men. Mere numbers alone, he stated in *Art of War*, conferred no advantage. For a military man living in an age of constant violence, Sun Tsu had an extraordinary air of peace and tranquillity about him. He did not conceive war in terms of slaughter and destruction, but believed an objective should and could be taken with the proper use of strategy and sound information of the enemy's plans. His prime directive was that 'the skilful strategist should be able to subdue the enemy's army without engaging it, take his cities without laying siege to them, and overthrow his State without bloodying swords'. He always cautioned his emperor not to place reliance on sheer military power. Being a staunch advocate of espionage and covert operations he counselled that to use his tactics would contribute to a speedy outcome of an impending war. This highly informative book on waging war, being well known to the wandering priests of the time, was instrumental in the birth of what was soon to be known as ninjutsu.

Forest demons

In the vast woodlands of northern China, bands of robbers existed in great numbers. One of these robber groups lived in the very heart of the forest. On their travels the priests often sought refuge and shelter for the night with these bands of brigands, who were called by the simple Chinese peasants *lin kui* or forest demons. The lin kui had learned to survive with nature in harmony and everything they needed to live was gleaned from the vast forests. Food, shelter, clothes, all were obtained from their natural habitat. They only ventured into the civilized world to earn money either by robbing or hiring themselves out to local warlords to spy on possible enemies. It would seem only natural then that over the years the travelling priests picked up much information of how these lin kui lived and survived.

Severe internal problems within China at this time led to many bloody revolts. Scholars and priest alike fell from royal favour and patronage at the Sui dynasty (ad 589–618) court. Consequently, many intellectuals had to flee their homeland and seek refuge in Japan.

Masters of the Occult

Unlike their Buddhist counterparts, these Taoist priests had for centuries delved into the mystic teachings and Shamanistic aspects of their religion. Much of this was developed from the esoteric knowledge of Tibet and India. Black magic arts, alchemy, longevity procedures via specialized breathing and meditation exercises had been practised by these priests and handed down from master to student for generations. Home to many of these practitioners of the 'secret arts' were caves and mountain top retreats far away from prying eyes and the Emperor's soldiers. From dawn to dusk, year in and year out the priests put their bodies through all types of agonies in the pursuit of becoming at one with the Universe. Expanded consciousness and personal mind control aided by roots and herbal concoctions put the priests on a different intellectual and physical level from most other mortals. These cultivated states of mind expansion, harnessed with deep meditative procedures, enabled the priests to live in austere surroundings, in harmony with the beasts that shared their isolated existence.

Obviously to the uncultured and superstitious mind endurance practices such as controlled breathing and shallow breath techniques led the peasants to believe the priests could die and then come alive again.

Born of Blood

So tales of invulnerability sprang up and the local populace gave them a wide berth. They were regarded as almost superbeings. It was not unusual for traders to carry stories of these strange beings who lived on fresh air, were permanently in touch with heaven, and could talk and live at one with animals. The Emperor's court soon got to hear about these mountain priests and, rather than holding their achievements in awe, a great fear permeated the palace as the Emperor began to envisage the unrest such people could spread among his political enemies. Edicts were quickly sent out ordering on pain of death no one to aid or assist these priests. And any priests of this black art sect found wandering out in the open away from his mountain retreat were to be slain immediately. Officers of the army were warned that unless they were killed on sight the priests may work their magic and spirit themselves away. The Emperor further ordered that after the priest had been killed his body had to be burned to stop him rising from the dead.

To the uneducated mind belief in superstition made any story fact. This was a particular psychological penchant the ninja would put to good use in the centuries to come. With such persecution the many various Taoist mountain ascetics thought it both prudent and tactical to leave their country and search for a new home in another land. So they sought sanctuary in the islands of Japan. They took with them all the knowledge they had accumulated over the centuries as well as their scrolls which contained the secret doctrines and formulae. This wealth of occult information gleaned from decades of meditative practice and experimentation was lost to China for ever.

First espionage agents

Upon arrival in their new land the dissidents, especially the priests, settled in remote mountainous areas around the provinces of Iga and Koga, little knowing that they were soon to be disturbed by events that were taking place in the Japanese political arena. The Prince Regent of Japan at that time was Shotoku, a fervent Buddhist who was engaged in a battle for succession to the throne with an usurper named Moriya. Shotoku, on the advice of the Buddhist priests who had gained access to the royal Japanese court through religious influence, employed men to spy and gather information on his rival. This was the first authenticated account of espionage agents ever being used in Japan.

When Shotoku finally became ruler he promulgated Buddhism above all other religions and for a time Japan's own indigenous religion of Shinto had to take a back seat. For 30 years Buddhism flourished under Shotoku until his death in AD 622. Then the various religious factions became embroiled in a bloodthirsty power struggle over which doctrine should be designated as the state religion. The struggle soon got out of hand and began to involve everybody. Such was the disorder, that the country began to suffer great stress both governmentally and economically. However, a man came forward in the guise of a saviour. He was En-no-Gyoja, a mountain warrior ascetic or priest that the Japanese people called *yamabushi* (warrior priest). Trying to solve the dispute and restore order he promoted a different form of Buddhism called Shugendo. This new religion quickly gained much support from the people and became very popular. However, it was inevitable that the court aristocracy and the rich landowners would fear that En-no-Gyoja and his followers were gaining too much power. To force a showdown the various petty officials mustered a huge army and sent it out to defeat En-no-Gyoja.

Mountain stronghold of the yamabushi

Greatly outnumbered, the yamabushi were slaughtered in their hundreds. The few that remained beat a hasty retreat to the vast and remote mountainous regions of Iga on the island of Honshu in central Japan to lick their wounds. This desolate area was shrouded in mists, the mountain paths were barely accessible and few people ever ventured there. It was the ideal location for the yamabushi to regroup and eventually settle. For a time many other political refugees, dissidents, persecuted Taoist and Buddhist priests on the run, wandered into the isolated area seeking refuge in the yamabushi encampments. Gradually, over a period of about 400 years, the huge encampments split into clans. Whole families began to emerge through intermarriage, and from the few hundred original yamabushi and Chinese Taoist priests grew clans which numbered in their thousands.

In total isolation, generation after generation of yamabushi lived, worked and died. Every skill that they possessed was put to good and effective use. The military treatise *Art of War* was studied, assimilated and then applied, its advice being effective when snooping imperial soldiers entered the mountains in search of escaped political prisoners. Many of these imperial search parties, once they had strayed into the Iga region, were never seen again.

The yamabushi raised families and studied the teachings and philosophies of Buddhism and Taoist alchemy practices. Within the framework of Shugendo Buddhism is a sect called *Shingon* (true word). Shingon is heavily influenced by Tantric beliefs and dwells much on mysticism. Central to Shingon belief is 'Dainichi', a Buddha whose name means Buddha of infinite light. To the followers of

Born of Blood

Shingon, Dainichi is the source of all existence, absolute and permanent. Certain occult rites are practised in Shingon, termed 'Mikkyo', meaning secret knowledge. The Mikkyo constituted teachings involving worship of the spirits of nature (which well suited the yamabushi in their mountain wilderness) and also magic, meditation, and most importantly unlocking the secrets of the human mind. These religious practices were aimed at uniting human mental powers with supernatural forces for the purpose of interpreting the secrets of the universe.

Mystical training

Influenced by Tibetan Tantric principles and Indian yoga systems the yamabushi devised a method for concentrating all their will and energy into one endeavour at any given moment. This was initiated by employing hand signs involving intricate finger-knitting patterns termed *kuji-in* (energy channelling). Kuji-in was the base for what are known as the five manifestations, which are earth, fire, wind, water, and void. These five hand positions were the primers for a further number resulting in 81 positions in all.

The 81 finger-entwining hand positions are able to cover any circumstance in which the ninja may find himself. By calming his mind and adopting a kuji-in hand manoeuvre the ninja in a semi-trance-like state could induce all manner of physiological changes within his own body. These included being able to slow down his heartbeat and reduce blood pressure, apply maximum concentration upon any given problem, stay awake with full faculties for amazing lengths of time, and hold his breath for at least three minutes or more. The kuji-in helped the ninja adopt the best frame of mind for whatever venture he was involved in. The mystical training in Mikkyo also aided the ninja to increase his own god-given usual five senses, long meditative practices developing his inherent powers of psychic perception. All of these capabilities, and more, created havoc among the superstitious feudal peasants, as we shall see. So important is the mental awareness aspect of the Mikkyo teachings that even today ninjutsu training involves the development of such powers.

The golden age of ninjutsu

The centuries rolled by and little was heard from the rebellious mountain priests, ordinary folk thinking that they had long since perished in desolation. At the end of the Heian period, in 1185, the Japanese central government had become so weak that many factions among the aristocracy were at work wheeling and dealing. Constant conflicts between lords and religious leaders, all vying for power, provided

A Hokusai woodblock print depicting the early use of taijutsu.
At top right a ninja can be seen scaling up a wall on a rope.

the perfect setting for the use of spies and assassins to eliminate political adversaries. Thus dawned a time of political unrest called the Kamakura Period (1192-1333), which also became known as 'the golden age of ninjutsu'. With all this power-mongering taking place, utilizing the ninja and their special talents, which were well known to a few *Daimyo* (lords), seemed the ideal solution for the feuding officials to call upon in an effort to rid them of opponents. It was during the Kamakura Period that the military dictatorship known as the Shogunate was born, the emperor merely being a figurehead for the country. Along with the Shogunate came the rise to power of the Samurai warriors, and their own religion called Zen Buddhism, which laid the foundation for the whole of the Samurai culture. Yet culturally the Samurai and the ninja were at opposite ends of the scale.

Because of the many private armies that were being organized by the provincial barons, information about troop movements and military strengths and weaknesses was in great demand. The rich lords ruled their areas, making up laws as they went along, leaving their faithful Samurai to ensure they were carried out. Consequently, the use of ninja spies became more and more commonplace. For their part, the ninja espionage tactics resulted in the right information reaching the right ears. The lords soon found that one or two agents in the enemy encampment were cheap and that they learned more than a whole army of Samurai could glean. Under the cover of darkness or disguised as a wandering priest the ninja moved freely about the enemy's stronghold gathering information about everything. Within a short space of time the ninja became essential for intelligence work – and soon progressed from information gathering to assassination.

Birth of the shadow warrior

Various military generals figured that if a ninja agent could penetrate deep behind the enemy lines, gain access to a camp or castle and then silently slay the army commander or Daimyo himself, then that particular foe would be leaderless and consequently vanquished, without their armies ever having to meet on the battlefield. This implied a great saving both economically and in terms of human lives. Thus the ninja night assassin, the shadow warrior, was born.

During this 'golden age', the ninja clans blossomed into as many as 70 distinct *ryu* (schools), with the main strongholds centred in the areas of Iga and Koga provinces. In those days the ninja were known as *shinobi* or stealers-in. Each of the ninja family clans was characterized by its own particular brand of espionage and use of certain weaponry. These specialities were closely guarded secrets, and each member of a family handed these down through the generations only to members of their own family. For example, a technique known as *koppojutsu*, which specialized in bone-breaking, was a particular favourite of the Koto clan. The Fudo family were expert in, and responsible for, the development of the star-shaped throwing implement called *shuriken*. Espionage on an elaborate scale was the hallmark of the Kusonoki clan, and later, the great clan of Togakure were adept with the *shuko* and *tetsubishi* (climbing claws and caltrops). In Iga province the two biggest families were Hattori and Oe, who ruled the ninja jointly while to the north in Koga province the clans of Mochizuki, Ukai and Nakai ruled.

By the 14th century the ninjutsu organizations had grown in huge numbers, and had become great influential and political adversaries of the government. They were no longer content to remain in obscurity in the wilderness and mountains, so they emerged *en masse* and assassinated the Daimyo that were against them, easily defeating their various armies. The very name of the ninja began to strike fear in the hearts of the aristocracy of the time. The Ashikaga family had seized control of Japan and a period of total disorganization followed. Warfare was rife between rival factions, almost to the point of rebellion and civil war. Groups of nobles and powerful

Born of Blood

Samurai families fought one another for positions of power. Inevitably, by 1500 all of Japan was engulfed by civil war, the country having lost most of its central government due to weak and easily influenced Shoguns. In effect the Daimyo had taken over, each one possessing a self-governing territory in which the ruling lord made all the laws. The next hundred years saw the ninja clans infiltrating all areas of finance and government. To many, the ninja seemed to be getting completely out of hand. It was said that they had even set their sights on the capital itself.

The ninjas' dreaded enemy

At this point a great military general, who had ideas himself of becoming the Shogun, appeared on the scene. This was Oda Nobunaga, the dreaded hater and avowed enemy of all ninja. Nobunaga's rise to power seemed to have come almost unnoticed. He had been a petty lord, a minor Daimyo, then general of a whole army. Aided by his allies he proclaimed himself Shogun, and moved into the capital Kyoto. Nobunaga was a fierce and heartless ruler with an excessively cruel streak that resulted in him going on the rampage and declaring war on the Buddhists. He had earlier aligned himself with the new Christian movement that had arrived in Japan some years before via the Jesuits. Although not the slightest bit religious himself, Nobunaga thought that by wiping out the many warlike Buddhist sects he could gain total control of the country. Also, one of the biggest threats at that time was the Shingon Buddhists, who were of course the ninja. In 1571, Nobunaga was responsible for the massacre on Mount Hiei, where with 30,000 troops he put to the sword over 100,000 men, women and children, and razed completely to the ground this ancient religious dwelling place and centre. For over five years Nobunaga was the scourge of Japan. He massacred and burnt down anything connected with Buddhism. His huge army had gained almost total control of Japan, and slowly the many Daimyo offered him their allegiance, mainly out of fear rather than liking. Nobunaga's army was the best equipped and most advanced in the country, mainly due to the number of European muskets it possessed, brought in by the Dutch and Portuguese traders who had arrived with the Jesuits.

Fear in the soul

But still, Nobunaga's greatest fear was that of the ninja clans. Legend relates that his fear arose through an incident in his early life. Nobunaga was out on a hunting trip with a few of his retainers. His travels had taken him into the remote Iga region, heartland of the ninja. Suddenly his horse threw him to the ground.

There, in the eerie stillness of the fog-enshrouded forest, he is said to have felt a fear that rooted itself in his very soul. For a few silent moments the myths and tales of the dreaded faceless warriors of the night, the ninja, seemed all too apparent. Although no one was around, he felt totally unprotected and at their mercy. Swiftly climbing back into the saddle he sped away taking with him this haunting fear.

Many years later, yet still obviously psychologically disturbed by this experience, Nobunaga called to his side his son Katsuyori to lead the army into Iga province and wipe out the ninja clans. In 1579 a vast army of Samurai under the leadership of Katsuyori set out to attack the ninja clans. As for the ninja themselves, although outnumbered their clever tactical strategy and guerrilla hit-and-run manoeuvres caused many problems for Katsuyori's army. They finally met head-on in the great battle of Tensho Iga no Ram. The ninja forces proved to be far too clever for the Samurai. Using all their ingenuity and warfare skills the ninja soundly beat the invading force and Katsuyori's army retreated with huge losses.

Slaughter of the ninja

This defeat only added fuel to Nobunaga's nervous apprehension of the ninja and two years later in 1581 he made a determined effort in a 'once and for all' bid to wipe out the dreaded black assassins. He personally led a massive force of over 46,000 men to saturate the Iga hinterland with Samurai, including crack regiments of musket men – all expert marksmen. Nobunaga's armies outnumbered the ninja clans by more than ten to one and this time Nobunaga was victorious, his sheer overwhelming forces putting the ninja clans on the run. Nobunaga's orders were that everyone should be slaughtered. The ninja losses of men, women and children were staggering. Almost all of the Iga clan was wiped out. The few that managed to escape fled even deeper into the mountains. Here they regrouped and began the slow process of training new warriors in the skills of the ninja. Even so, the once-powerful ninja clans had had their heyday.

A year later the hated Oda Nobunaga was murdered while travelling through Honhiji territory. Some say that an isolated group of ninja carried out the deed in retaliation for the slaughter of their families. After the death of Nobunaga two generals vied for the leadership. It was eventually decided that Nobunaga's first favourite, a general named Hideyoshi Toyotomi, would rule. One of Hideyoshi's first acts was to prohibit peasants from owning or carrying weapons. He even went as far as to stop the population from changing their occupations, which eventually led to the end of social mobility. Unlike

Born of Blood

Nobunaga, Hideyoshi despised the Christians and their converts. In 1597 he began a persecution campaign against them, and like his predecessor had behaved towards the Buddhists, Hideyoshi massacred the Christians in their thousands. Hideyoshi saw foreign interference and influence (mostly from the West) as counterproductive to his aim of a united Japan.

Returning a vital favour

Meanwhile the second favourite of Nobunaga, a general named Tokugawa Ieyasu, had been posted to a castle in the east of the country. For him to get to his newly appointed position he had to travel through the treacherous mountain passes in Iga. The thought of journeying through ninja territory after the events of the previous years didn't appeal to Ieyasu. So in a clever strategical move, he approached a leading ninja clan chief named Hanzo Hattori for guidance and protection in return for future favours. Hattori saw in this situation a chance to gain power so he agreed. The ninja chieftain sent out word to the Iga and Koga ninja that Ieyasu's caravan was not to be harmed or stopped, as Hattori himself would be leading it. All the ninja complied with the request and Ieyasu was afforded safe passage. This one act by the ninja leader was to prove very beneficial at a later date.

Exactly one year after the massacre of the Christians Hideyoshi realized that he had created an almost military caste in the country, giving birth to the rise and power of the Samurai. He found that the feudal lords and Daimyo were starting revolts. The edict issued about carrying arms had caused uprisings and made the collection of local taxes very difficult. All this had begun to interfere with Hideyoshi's expansion plans, and in 1598 the great general died. This event had a monumental effect upon the ninja clans. Hideyoshi's successor was Tokugawa Ieyasu, who quickly established himself in control. He set about quelling all the revolts and subduing the Daimyo. To do this he needed a vast network of espionage agents to inform him of what was going on around the country. This is when the favour by ninja clan chief Hanzo Hattori was returned. The Iga ninja began a large-scale operation, infiltrating castles, forts, and all military establishments outside the new capital of Edo (Tokyo), reporting back news and events to Ieyasu about dissident nobles. Thus Hanzo Hattori found himself elevated into the higher echelons of power inside the government.

Peace – and loss of ninja power

Ieyasu, using the ninja agents effectively, reduced insurrection to nil. During this period the shadow warriors were kept very busy spying and carrying out direct assassinations against the feudal lords that would not comply with Ieyasu's dictates. Thus the ninja once again plied their deadly trade with swift justice to all who stood in the way of Ieyasu and the Shogunate. In 1603 Ieyasu assumed the title of Shogun at Edo. There now followed a series of edicts that had dramatic effects upon Japan, and ironically led to the eventual demise of the ninja as a powerful force.

This period in history became known as the Tokugawa Shogunate. Ieyasu blocked the earlier trade expansion with the West by closing off the country to foreigners. All the ports were shut, except for a small trading post at Nagasaki, run by the Dutch. He ordered that the central government divide the country into 250 feudal areas, each ruled by an over-lord. These lords were required to spend a month each year in the capital at Edo. This was done to reduce the possibility of conspiracy. As long as the lords remained loyal to the Shogun they were free to operate as they pleased. For the next 260 years Japan became isolated from the rest of the world, and for the first time in centuries civil order was restored and the country was united and at peace.

Unfortunately for the ninja, this peace sealed their end as a dominating power. Hanzo Hattori and his family remained in the employ of the Shogun, pro-tecting the Shogunate. Hattori organized his ninja into a secret police force and spy system so that Tokugawa Ieyasu could be aware of dissidents and political agitators long before they could ever amount to becoming a threat. The odd ninja or two dispatched at the right time could get rid of any would-be usurpers. But for the mainstay of the ninja clans the peaceful times meant that their work dried up.

So the deadly ninja that had been feared for almost ten centuries throughout Japan became little more than gardeners and security guards, their own skills declining along with their art. Many melted into the community doing jobs that their skills best equipped them for. Others found work as farm labourers and put aside the skills of war. The few ninja that couldn't exist in civilian life wandered high into the mountains in pursuit of religious activities. Consequently the ninja organizations broke up and disbanded – or so many people thought. A few small groups went underground and continued to practise their skills, handing down to each generation the ways and methods of ninjutsu.

Ninja versus the West

The next time Japan heard of the ninja was in 1853 when the United States sent Commodore Perry and his 'Black Ships' to Japan to open up the country as a trading route. The Shogun of the period sent two ninja on board the Western barbarians' ships to steal papers and gain information of what they were really up to. The papers that were stolen proved to be totally insignificant and can be seen today on display in a Tokyo museum. When Japan adopted the open-door policy for trading, the inevitable flood from the West brought new science and technology to the Japanese. A proper training programme for an army and navy was instigated, Samurai were forbidden to wear swords, and feudal Japan entered the 20th century. In little more than 40 years Japan had caught up with the rest of the world. In the early 1900s Japan had an altercation with the mighty bear of Russia, who had taken Port Arthur. It is without doubt that the Japanese secret service had full knowledge of the exploits of the ninja from long ago, and using their espionage and covert activity methods were successful at gaining pre-knowledge of the strengths and weaknesses of their Russian enemy. They attacked the Russian fleet and were successful; thus again the tactics of the ancient ninja helped win the day. Many people thought that Japan's act of a surprise attack on Port Arthur was not quite fair, as Japan did not declare war on Russia until the next day. But the art of the ninja is the art of winning. Perhaps if they had formally declared their intentions to the Russians, the outcome would have been entirely different.

Into the 20th century

Surprisingly, not much is known or recorded about the ninja after the Russo-Japanese war until the late 1960s. In the first few decades of the 20th century Japan set about a world and trade expansion, which involved them invading China and completely overrunning Manchuria. For such widespread military operations it would be more than reasonable to assume that the tried and tested methods of the ancient ninja were put to full use. Bearing in mind the ninjas' ingenuity for adapting anything and everything as a weapon, one can only wonder to what use they put the advanced technology of the 1920s and 1930s.

It is known that vast espionage networks were established by the Japanese throughout Manchuria, and certain dissenting Chinese warlords mysteriously disappeared when any kind of contention arose. In the true traditions of the ancient ninja, agents were dispatched to Manchuria long before the Japanese invasion. These spies, acting as a kind of fifth column, would settle in Chinese towns and villages, gaining employment in all walks of Chinese life. They reported anything that might be of interest to the Japanese secret service, in an effort to make the impending invasion run more smoothly. Such information included troop strengths in certain areas, location of munitions factories and supply routes, the mood of the people, how best to use propaganda as a weapon – in fact anything at all that could somehow be used for subversion.

Heavily involved with Japanese secret service activities around that time was an organization called the Black Dragon Society, also known as the Amur River Society. This society was founded in 1901, when the nationalists were convinced that Japan would have to fight Russia. One of its activities was espionage in Manchuria and Siberia. It was fitting, therefore, that it should call itself the 'Amur River Society'. The Chinese characters for 'Amur', translated literally, mean Black Dragon. The man usually credited with the founding of this society in the early part of this century is Mitsuru Toyama although it has been suggested that its early beginnings stem from a ninja clan that went underground some 200 years previously. Unfortunately due to the very nature of ninja activity and organization, little has been documented – and even less is known – about such groups as the Black Dragon and its contemporary, the 'Zaijari' which had off-shoots into the infamous Triad societies.

It seems a strange paradox that although history can recall many of the ninja clans exploits up until around 1650, any information after that time seems to be non-existent. But then a secret once told ceases to be a secret. And a ninja once discovered ceases to be effective. So it would seem only reasonable to assume that, given the advent of modern communications and espionage methods, the ninjas' pathological need for secrecy went even deeper. We have only to look at their Western counterparts in the CIA and MI5. If their every covert activity was documented and made public knowledge, these organizations would cease to be effective almost immediately.

So to all intents and purposes history would have us believe that the ninja clans ceased to function as an organization with the coming of the Tokugawa Shogunate. However, to accept this as fact would be naive. A foundation of nearly a thousand years' experience in espionage, covert activities and political assassination – not to mention a huge, well-oiled propaganda machine that was constantly in use to keep the common people in check by fear tactics – just would not be wasted simply because a time of peace prevailed.

Let us go back to Sun Tsu's *Art of War*, which points out that through a well-laid-out and well-placed espionage system a government can be overthrown without the bloodying of swords. This book is also known as *The 13 Chapters* and in thirteen short essays upon the waging of war SunTsu offers every known (at the time of writing) scenario and then some, on overcoming an enemy force. This book is so succinct in its treatise on warfare that today it is required first-year reading in every military and officers' training academy in the world.

Art of War purports to work on the ancient universal laws of war and its underlying theme stresses the importance of calculations by the use of strategy. It could be a veritable bible for covert operators such as the ninja. Sun Tsu points out the relationships between war and factors of politics, economics, diplomacy, geography, and most important of all, the use of spies. It is with this theory on the use of covert operators in the enemy camp or stronghold that *Art of War* comes into its own. As Sun Tsu states, 'All warfare is based upon deception.' And the premise, 'My enemy's enemy is my friend', allowed the ninja to make great use of double agents and the 'mole' aspect of espionage. Sun Tsu stated that spies are the most important element in war, because on them an army's ability to move rests. An army without spies is like a man without eyes or ears.

Thus there is little doubt that Hanzo Hattori's early work of setting up a nationwide government espionage system with his ninja clans for Tokugawa Ieyasu heralded the beginning of a highly organized Japanese secret service. We can only conjecture to what extent the ninja were employed in World War II. It has even been suggested by some contemporary martial arts historians that the plans to assassinate General MacArthur were ninja inspired.

Secret Art of the Ninja

Ninja lives today

In the 1980s the martial arts world has seen a great revival of the arts of the ninja. Unfortunately in the 1960s, before the West could establish the credibility of ninjutsu as a martial art, commercialism reared its head, saw the potential of this ancient warrior caste, and began to market in a sensational way its ancient forms of assassination and subversion. The greatly exaggerated exploits of the ninja agent on film and television gave rise to the true ninja arts being held up to a certain amount of ridicule within world martial arts circles. Then in the early 1970s the efforts of two men, Doron Navon from Israel and Stephen K. Hayes from the United States, who both trained to instructor level in Japan, gave this once black art the official seal of approval in the West.

Both these Western pioneers of ninjutsu trained under Japanese ninja master Dr Masaaki Hatsumi – the 34th grandmaster of what has been described as the oldest remaining historically traceable ninja organization in the world, the Togakure Ryu Ninja. Grandmaster Hatsumi inherited his title from the 33rd grandmaster, Toshitsugu Takamatsu, upon the latter's death. It is only through the efforts of Dr Hatsumi that ninjutsu became known to the Western world, since until the death of his own master the art of ninjutsu was kept totally underground as a secret tradition and only taught to students privately. Another ninja clan, that of the Koga Ryu Ninja, is also said to exist and still be training in the warrior arts. But if this is true then they are maintaining the tradition of their ancestors by remaining strictly secret and underground. Koga ninja instructors openly teach in the West, but a central point of Japanese instructional reference has never yet been created.

How many other ninja organizations are in existence is anyone's guess. Secrecy, after all, is still at the heart of the ninja.

Training to Kill

The pursuit of excellence is a lifelong endeavour

IN historical terms the *shinobi* or ninja warrior inherited his profession at birth. The young ninja started his apprenticeship in the arts of stealth and mayhem almost from the cradle. From their earliest years, the children of ninja families were conditioned to be constantly aware of everything around them, the laws of nature being their permanent companions. For by being tuned in, as it were, to natural events and phenomena, a greater understanding of the elements could be developed. This knowledge could then be put to good use to effect either an escape or evasion tactic or as a psychological weapon against the superstitious peasants, who deemed even a simple eclipse of the sun as some form of evil portent from the *kami* (gods).

Deadly games

From about the age of four or five, ninja children's games were centred around serious training exercises. A child's abilities were carefully observed and then tested to see if they had any inborn skills or special traits. Those with talent were nurtured to hone their inherent skills to almost epic proportions. This is similar to modern-day Soviet athletes who are taken at an early age and rigorously trained for years to achieve peak Olympic performances. All the ninja childhood games stressed subtle training points that, although not immediately evident, would prove to be most important at a later date in their lives. Games that encouraged balance and agility were at the top of the list. Running up inclined planks and leaping over low bushes, or hanging from the branches of trees by their arms for hours on end, taught them the feeling of pain and at the same time how to maintain a strong sense of self-discipline.

In the ninja encampments, which resembled small villages, experts were on hand in every conceivable skill to teach and train the ninja children. These instructors would have more than likely been field ninja that at one time or another had either injured themselves or been maimed during a mission and yet survived. Every morning and evening the children's young muscles, although still only gristle, would be worked upon by experts in massage to keep their bones and joints flexible. This was done so that in later life, out in the field on a mission, should they be captured and tied up, a simple disjointing of the limb would effect an immediate release and escape to freedom. Massage in Eastern countries, especially in Japan, has usually been the domain of women. So it is more than likely that the female ninja, known as *kunoichi*, were the ones that carried out this task.

Freedom to train and fight

Each year in the life of a child ninja some other skill was added to their already greatly expanding repertoire of techniques. It is difficult for us in the West to conceive the continuous training programme of a ninja. Morning, noon – and well into the night – the ninja children trained and trained in an effort to reach as near perfection as possible. To try to understand the thinking behind this intensive training regime we must remember the times that the ninja lived in. Feudal Japan was oppressed and the state dictated everything. Unless of noble birth, the average Japanese could only expect a life of toil and austerity, where the slightest affront to anyone of a higher station could mean instant death. Examined in these terms, perhaps the life of a ninja wasn't quite as bad as that of his counterpart, the feudal farmer working in the fields from dawn to dusk. At least the ninja had the freedom of the forests and mountains, with all the security of belonging to a family unit.

A classical training exercise for ninja children, which aimed at developing their stamina and which produced the ability to run swiftly, was that of speed-travelling. This involved the use of a peasant's straw hat, which was placed on the child's chest as the young ninja set off running. If he could keep the hat pressed firmly up against his chest by the force of the wind only, through running very fast, then that was enough for his teachers to advance the young ninja to a higher level of training. The ninja agent had to be a superior runner, not only to elude pursuers but also to carry important intelligence reports which they had gathered, back to their superiors. It must be pointed out that in feudal Japan horses were not freely available: it was usually only the nobles and high-ranking military who were seen on horseback. A mounted horseman other than the two types mentioned, would more than likely bring too much attention to himself – and that's the last thing any ninja agent would want to do. Good strong legs and unlimited stamina would give the ninja field agent an effective retreat avenue. It is said that a ninja could run more than 50 miles non-stop in one day. This may seem an awesome feat, but bear in mind that it is only twice the distance of a modern-day marathon, and many people find no difficulty with that. Add to this the fact that the ninja trained for around 18 years to accomplish these amazing feats of stamina, and this accomplishment at 50 miles a day doesn't seem too daunting or unbelievable.

Superhuman shadow warriors

Constant body conditioning and training brought the ninja warrior up to a maximum peak of fitness and physical endurance, and it is easy to understand why the simple country folk thought that these shadow warriors were almost superhuman. Continuous daily training without let-up, sustained and carefully monitored diet, expert training in armed and unarmed combat skills, residing in the safety of a family unit during their formative years, and living at one with nature, were ideal ingredients for producing a race of superhumans. The ninja's finely honed skills and powers enabled them to squeeze through near-impossible openings, hold their breath for very long periods underwater, swim vast distances at high speed, and dive from great heights off cliff tops.

Mountain lakes were where young ninja students learned all the tricks necessary to gain entrance to a castle to carry out their missions. They were trained to move through the water silently with scarcely a ripple to be seen. The young ninja also practised fighting, with and without weapons, in the water. Water-evasion techniques became just another speciality in the arsenal of acquired skills for the ninja. A ninja knew exactly to what depth he must swim underwater to avoid the arrows of his pursuers, and in later years the musket balls of the rifleman.

Breathing and breath control, which the ninja had learned from childhood, were based on Indian yoga systems. It seems likely that the methods came to Japan via China, brought there by the Taoist mystics who spent all their lives experimenting with elaborate breathing techniques in their quest for immortality. To a ninja, the ability to suppress his breathing capabilities was useful in many ways. For example, when a ninja went into hiding, especially near a position occupied by the enemy, the slightest sound, if detected, may well have proven to be his last. If the soldiers' dogs were near, even inhaling and exhaling could prove fatal. Many stories abound in Japanese folklore of how the ninja escaped by using their method of shallow breathing to feign death. Some ninja even reduced their breathing by entering into a yoga-type hypnotic trance.

Alertness equalled survival

Throughout all ninja training the one constant that remained uppermost was the necessity to gain the

Training to Kill

'edge'. For by always having a great knowledge of the enemy and his capabilities the ninja could fall back on his training and handle each situation with a set course of procedure and action. The field ninja lived on his wits, and was constantly alert within his environment. Consequently, everyday happenings that most people just took for granted could mean an awful lot to the astute ninja agent.

By being trained to recognize a myriad of sounds without actually ever seeing the person or object making that sound, the ninja could detect impending danger. By being able to assess any noise he heard, such as a door being opened or closed, or footsteps heard in the distance, he could judge not only in which direction they were coming from but also the type of person he had to deal with. The swish of leather against bamboo, heard however softly, could perhaps indicate that a Samurai was approaching and the sound of the leather thongs on his armour pressing against the Samurai's breastplate would have prepared the ninja for a surprise assault.

As the ninja child reached his formative years he would be able to enter a room full of sleeping people and instantly judge, by listening to their breathing, how many bodies were in the room. To the trained ear the tell-tale rhythmic breathing of the sleeping people also enabled the ninja to distinguish a light or heavy sleeper, and a false sleeper from a genuine one. It is by being aware of even the most minute details that the ninja was able to slip quietly and unseen into the most fortified castles and strongholds and successfully accomplish his mission without detection.

Among the many skills in ninja training, none was more important that that of acting. For, like all spies, his very safety depended upon how well he could carry off the particular disguise format that he was adopting in his espionage quest, be it as a priest or merchant, or even a *ronin* (masterless Samurai). In feudal Japan, movement was very restricted, and Samurai border and boundary guards were stationed everywhere. It was an age of suspicion and insurrection and local Daimyo lived in constant fear of invading armies from other areas trying to overthrow them and take their lands as their own. If a traveller did not have a bona fide reason for being in an area he was either killed or taken prisoner. It was in this kind of atmosphere that the ninja agent had to try to ply his trade. So dressing up and looking like a priest or merchant just wasn't enough. They had to be completely proficient in the mannerisms and accomplishments of the people whose guise they had adopted. A wandering Buddhist or Shinto priest was usually welcome at all courts and castles. So a ninja in this guise would have to be expert in religious ceremonies and rites in order to carry off his disguise with success.

Training to Kill

To many people the time involved in learning the skills of ninjutsu seems extraordinarily long, but when you consider that the hundred and one things they had to master would in future save their lives on many occasions, then the time becomes irrelevant. They constantly updated techniques when new ideas and recent technical innovations were discovered. This updating included changes in both weaponry and warfare and also in civil advancements.

The 18 areas of expertise

At the height of the historical ninja period, the Togakure ninja clans were trained in 18 areas of expertise which progressed from basic weapon skills to more advanced realms of mental and psychic abilities. But always in ninja training the purity of the soul was most important, sometimes referred to as the 'ninja heart'. The 18 levels were:

1. Spiritual refinement, which involved the ninja coming to terms with his strengths and weaknesses, and intention, commitment and personal motivation. Being part philosopher through the mystical teachings of the Shugendo, the ninja strived to put himself in touch with the universal laws of nature.

2. Unarmed combat, involving grappling and escaping, plus rolling and leaping.

3. Ninja sword, involving fast-draw sword techniques and cutting and attacking.

4. Stick and staff fighting, involving use of 6 ft and 4 ft (1.8 m and 1.2 m) staffs and the *hanbo* (staff).

5. *Shuriken* (razor-sharp stars) throwing.

6. Spear fighting.

7. *Naginata* (spear) techniques, involving fighting with the halberd.

8. Chain and sickle weapons.

9. Fire and explosives, including demolition and distraction methods.

10. Disguise and impersonation, including personality traits and career roles.

11. Stealth and entering methods, combining silent movements with breaking and entering.

12. Horsemanship.

13. Water training, involving swimming and floating.

14. Strategy, including unconventional tactics, deception, political plots and influencing events.

15. Espionage, including recruiting spies and setting up espionage cells.

16. Escape and concealment, involving camouflage and invisibility techniques.

17. Meteorology involving forecasting and taking advantage of the weather conditions.

18. Geography, including terrain features, mapmaking and combat strategy.

Training to Kill

Ninja children were brought up to become the perfect — or as near perfect as possible — killing machine. Only the mission mattered, all else was unimportant. Their total devotion to this aim knew no bounds. This was instilled into them almost from the time they could comprehend the spoken word. Each skill learned brought them a step nearer to becoming a total warrior, able to survive the hardships of harsh weather, fight off the enemy who were sometimes three and four strong, withstand great pain under torture (if they were captured), and yet never divulge anything they knew — even to the point of committing suicide rather than betray the clan.

The art of stealth

The name Shinobi means stealing-in or stealth art. It is taken from the Japanese written character, and it is from this word that ninjutsu was derived. So a ninja had to be expert in creeping around stealthily. For without a sound an assassin could become almost invisible, able to move about the old wooden castles of Japan with their creaking floorboards, yet never be discovered. In order to perfect those talents, ninja training devised certain techniques of walking. For instance in a movement known as *yoko aruki*, they learnt to walk by moving their legs sideways in a cross-step fashion. Tracks left in this manner do not readily reveal in which direction a ninja is travelling and thus confuse a pursuing enemy.

Ninja children, almost from the time they took their first steps, were taught to tread carefully and lightly. This training would often begin by them having to walk repeatedly through a shallow pool of water without making a splash and barely a ripple. Another method used when the children became older and more advanced, was to lay wet rice paper on the floor, on which the ninja students were required to walk up and down without the soles of their feet ripping or tearing the paper.

As training continued in its never-ending series of learning, the ninja was taught how to read simple maps and gain the skill of actual map-making. This was necessary because, apart from the assassinations the ninja carried out, espionage, spying andgleaning information of troop movements were very much part and parcel of his everyday field of activities. For this intelligence work to be carried out effectively, the ninja had to be able to sketch maps accurately indicating the terrain, the deployment of troops and the enemy's position in general in relation to the area in which they were camped.

Sometimes a ninja would be employed to create a diversion and slow down an advancing enemy, which was relatively easy for him to accomplish. A simple trick of poisoning the water that the horses drank

Training to Kill

would create catastrophic consequences, and hold up an advancing army long enough for the hunters to become hunted themselves. This kind of fifth-column activity was the hallmark of the ninja field warrior.

Psychological weapons

As the ninja children's knowledge accumulated, so too did their lessons. With age came comprehension and understanding, and the subtleties of human nature were explored in the ninja's advanced psychology classes. Obviously lessons of this nature had to be left until the children were of an age to appreciate how to use another man's greed or jealousy to find out information and *kunoichi* (female ninja) were taught how to use their charms in more amorous ways. It was important for the ninja to be skilled in the use of dialects, since one of the biggest give-aways would be when a ninja, operating far from his base, suddenly began to converse in a dialect that was alien to the particular part of the country in which he was operating. This danger would be heightened if the ninja's standard line of conversation didn't correspond with his disguise. The absolutely vast number of skills learned in the 18 to 20 years a ninja trained can only be measured by the continuing success they had as assassins and espionage agents for a thousand years.

Power of darkness

Although much has been written about the ninja only fighting at night, much of their work was actually done in the hours of daylight. As information-gatherers they would wander around village markets picking up on any conversation that would have aided them in their ultimate mission. However, gaining entry into a castle was obviously best left to the twilight hours. The military governing powers prohibited all movement by the common people in the hours of darkness, so at least the ninja knew that any sounds or gathering of people could only be soldiers or Samurai. Knowing this, and treating every noise as a potential danger to himself, he was well prepared for instant retaliation. With no light to guide him the ninja needed incredible night vision powers. It is therefore not unreasonable to assume that he ate vast amounts of watercress, which grew plentifully around the rivers and streams, to gain the valuable vitamin A for his eyesight. As a child the ninja would have to spend hours at a time in very small totally dark confines, in order to get his eyes used to the dark. Thus in later years, when out on assignments, he could operate with ease in the blackness of the night.

A ninja field agent would never fight just for fighting's sake. His whole aim was to get in, complete his mission, and then get out again without ever being seen. But even with the best-laid plans, the unexpected can happen. So, when confronted, the ninja had to fight his way out by whatever means possible. The skills he used in self-defence, both armed and unarmed, were truly awesome. Anything that came to hand became a weapon for the ninja to use in the protection of his life. A ninja's life was fraught with danger from dawn to dusk, from birth to grave. The more knowledgeable he became, the better his chances of surviving for the next assignment...

Invisible warriors

However, quite apart from being experts in all manner of combative arts the ninja, or the *genin*, (the agent in the field) looked upon using his fighting skills as failure of the mission. To move in and out and complete the mission without anyone being aware was the sole purpose of the agents. To be discovered and have to fight their way out of a situation meant that the Lords and generals who were being spied upon would be made aware that ninja activity was at large in their stronghold. Consequently blanket security and thorough searches would be made, even to the point of rewriting all their current planning operations in case the ninja had gathered the relevant information to take back. For all their rigid discipline Samurai generals were not stupid, and the consequences of a ninja at large in the camp would be absolutely catastrophic.

Discovery meant a failed mission for the ninja so it was of extremely important to follow his code of practice which was to be unseen, invisible and silent – to gather the information and be gone before the enemy had any idea their plans had been compromised. Some ninja missions could take weeks to accomplish so the ninja's masters would not be pleased with the report of a failed mission. To the ninja clan hired for the job at hand nothing mattered more than the success of the mission. The death of a genin was less important than the completion of the task or at least dying in the attempt to do so.

The five spy classes

Whenever possible the ninja field agents employed their years of training skills in espionage to infiltrate an enemy encampment or castle. Subtlety was their byword and drawing upon their childhood teachings they would employ one or more of the five classes of spying. These five classes were: local spies, inward spies, converted spies, doomed spies, and surviving spies. A local spy meant the ninja employed the services of an inhabitant of the district. An inward spy would mean the ninja had to make use of an official in the employ of his enemy. A converted spy would mean

As well as rope, steel claws were used for climbing. Even the thick ninja swordguard provided a footing when the scabbard was placed against a wall.

getting hold of the enemy's spies and using them for their own purpose. The latter is what we would today call a double agent. A doomed spy would be coerced or duped into serving the ninja on a mission by being captured or put to death by the enemy. For example, having captured a doomed spy, the enemy could be lulled into a false sense of security, believing they had caught a ninja in the performance of his mission. Once the doomed spy was put to death, the real ninja could then go about his espionage activities with a certain impunity.

Surviving spies were those who completed a mission and arrived back in their camp with all the required information. Sun Tsu classes the surviving spy as 'a man of keen intellect, though in outward appearance a fool; of shabby exterior but with a will of iron. He must be active, robust, endowed with physical strength and courage; thoroughly accustomed to all sorts of dirty work, able to endure hunger and cold, and to put up with shame and ignominy.'

A story is often told of a ninja who was sent on a mission to spy upon an adversary for the local Daimyo, taking note of the enemy's strength and troop movements. The ninja observed the encampment for a few days and noted all the comings and goings of military routine. He knew he had to get closer to find out more information so under the cover of darkness he sought out the hospital area of the camp and stealthily infiltrated the place where the sick troops were billeted. Quickly overcoming a sleeping patient he then donned the uniform of the man and made his way towards the central area where the Samurai officers were housed. Wandering around he listened in as the officers were selecting passwords and making plans. When enough knowledge of the enemy's intentions was gleaned he boldly strode over to where the horses were tethered, mounted up and calmly rode out of the camp.

As he passed the boundary of the camp he spied a soldier asleep on sentry duty. He stopped to remonstrate with him, giving him a sound scolding for putting the camp at the mercy of anyone passing. An officer, upon hearing the commotion, strolled across and joined the ninja in cursing the soldier for this very serious breach of discipline. The ninja nodded to the officer and rode off safely, with all the information needed to stop the enemy army dead in its tracks. As he rode off, he could still hear the officer shouting at the sentry for what he had done.

That story perhaps best exemplified the boldness and daring of the ninja agent in the execution of his mission. Fear did not become a factor in the equation because the ninja had no fear of death. This was not because he was stupid or regarded his life as expendable. It was the rigid training he had undergone from birth in mind control, psychology, and positive mental attitude that allowed the ninja to accomplish seemingly impossible tasks.

The Invisible Warrior

When they think you are near, be far.
When they think you are far, be near.

(Sun Tsu)

LIVING a rugged life as a social outcast the ninja learned to acclimatize his body to the weather of all the seasons and dressed accordingly. For instance, in the winter months he would don his garb of white so as to become virtually invisible in the snow. His brown-hued ninja suit in the autumn months would blend well with the falling leaves of the forest. Being able to blend in with his surroundings at any given moment fed the ninja legend over the years of his ability to disappear at will. The best hours of operation for the ninja who wished to remain unseen were naturally those of darkness, which permitted him to merge in with natural or other backgrounds. For very important and critical assignments, the ninja prepared his vision by keeping himself in the dark for at least 24 hours prior to his mission. His daylight hours would be spent deep in a dark cave, thus creating a fine night-sight sensitivity. It was this kind of cunning, deception and total dedication to his mission that often gave the ninja the edge over his enemies. For the ninja, however, being invisible did not necessarily entail not being seen, in the strict sense of the word. It also meant keeping his true intentions a secret and the ninja in disguise, acting as a travelling priest or merchant, was 'invisible' to his enemy

Planning a mission

The whole of the ninja clan structure centred around the success of the ninja field agent himself. These family systems were organized along strict military lines, with a hierarchy rather than a father, governing everything. The ninja were divided into three ranks: the *jonin* (the leaders); the *chunin* (the subleaders or lieutenants); and finally at the bottom of the scale the genin, the operational field agents, also known as ninja or shinobi.

The jonin maintained an extensive intelligence network. They made contact with the warlords and Daimyo who wanted subversive or espionage missions carrying out. Once the brief for the mission had been established, it would be given to a contact who had connections with a ninja clan. The contact then met the jonin concerned and the job was accepted.

All the necessary details would be ironed out between the jonin and the chunin. It was up to the chunin to select a genin or field ninja to go out and perform the task. As for the ninja agent himself, the fee for his services, or degree of impossibility of the task, were none of his concern. If selected, his only intention would be the 'mission' and its successful completion. Failure did not even enter into the genin's mind – he was either successful or killed; these were the only two options that existed. Bearing in mind this almost psychotic attitude to duty we can see how the ninja agent in execution of his mission must have been a frightening enemy.

For the ninja, being selected for his first mission would be the time when all his childhood training and the vast array of skills learned over the long years came into play. Because the ninja always planned ahead, knowing that for each situation he prepared for there would always be a dozen others he could never foresee, he would make sure he studied the geography of the mission area and its people. Once on his way the ninja would have selected the special weapons and tools he would need to complete the task. He would have prepared himself for the elements, depending upon the season. If, for instance, it was wintertime, his reversible suit would be worn on the white side, and he would wear heavy metal-bladed sandals to allow him to walk across frozen lakes and rivers. He would build a form of ice igloo to rest in and also plan his manoeuvres to fulfil his mission — and most importantly ensure that he had organized a suitable escape route. Often the ninja's ice house would be erected inside the branches of a low-hanging tree and in the direction of the prevailing wind. This facilitated a build-up of drifting snow which gave him extra cover as well as anonymity. In the more pleasant spring and autumn months, the ninja would dig himself a hole and cover it all over with earth, just leaving a small air hole to breathe through.

Focusing the mind on survival

The ninja field agent knew that survival was a state of mind. Correct planning meant that he would live to walk away. In the depths of winter, travelling across the wide open spaces with snow and ice all around and freezing winds chilling him to the marrow, many a lesser person would have just given up. But not the ninja. No matter how barren and bleak his predicament, through bringing into focus the powerful force of his mind and concentrating it on a given problem, he could quickly assess the right action to take in order to stay alive.

The Invisible Warrior

Making use of prevailing weather conditions was of prime importance to the ninja. Using the natural elements against the enemy gave him a very high advantage. The ability to recognize and predict weather conditions could sometimes make a lone ninja as effective as an army. If, for instance, the wind was blowing from a certain direction, he could gauge whether or not it was likely to change and with this knowledge would set fire to an enemy encampment knowing that the winds would blow towards the camp and fuel the fire even further. A huge army would soon be driven into chaos and confusion at the sight of a swiftly advancing mighty bush fire.

No weather conditions, no matter how severe they seemed, were ever deemed impossible for the ninja to work in. In fact, they welcomed any sort of unusual happenings, because the ninja always performed the unexpected. He took advantage of everything that came his way. Using deceptive ruses combined with good psychology, he flattered vain officials to cajole information from them. If the ninja was dressed as a priest, who in those days acted as news-bringers as well as religious leaders, he would have little difficulty in spreading lies of impending doom or pestilence to news-starved village communities. All this subversion was brilliantly executed — and it all worked to the ninja's benefit. He was invisible in the middle of the enemy, yet created an atmosphere of complete desperation all around him.

Because of a lifetime spent in outdoor training the ninja was adept at wisely using environmental camouflage to blend in with the terrain. His ingenious use of storms, fog and other natural phenomena terrified even the Samurai, who, although brave men against mortals, had no defence against what they thought were demons or ghosts.

Terror in the bravest heart

Once a ninja entered a castle, he knew that he would come up against light in one form or another, perhaps from the many oil-lamps hung around the Samurai barracks or from an open door in one of the castle apartments. So when light did appear at the place where he must enter or work in, the ninja took precautions against casting a tell-tale shadow. With an enemy potentially anywhere, each step he took had to be thought through. Problems were many, such as working upwind rather than downwind, lest the castle dogs caught his scent, or making sure an inadvertent sound was not magnified and carried to the castle sentries to alert them of his presence. The ninja's tricks and ruses were so diverse that even many of the nobles and lords thought that they were sorcerers or magicians who had control over nature. Superstitious villagers spoke about the ninja's occult powers in frightened whispers. Consequently, legends were built up to such an extent that the very mention of a ninja operating in their area struck terror into the bravest heart. The ninja worked on the premise that deception and surprise would lure the enemy into making false estimates and judgements, which would lead to erroneous military action. So, therefore, when an enemy was united, the ninja divided them; when the enemy was unprepared, the ninja attacked. By knowing how to wear an enemy down, how to keep him under constant strain, and by striking unseen and leaving no trace, it is not difficult to see why the ninja clans of Japan were held in such high esteem by the ruling lords of the period.

At the ninja's mercy

The Daimyo and lords were always aware that assassination attempts would be an almost regular occurrence. The more important or powerful the lord, then the more dangerous he was to an adversary. So in addition to having huge numbers of personal bodyguards who protected them at all times, they also rigged up little booby-traps in their living quarters as a second line of defence. These early alarm systems could detect an intruder within the private chambers of the castle and alert the Samurai guards. This meant that the ninja, once within the castle walls, had to run a gauntlet of both sophisticated and crude burglar alarms, such as doors deliberately left un-oiled so that if anyone tried to open one the creaking would be heard all around the halls. Always prepared, the ninja got around this by carrying a small phial of vegetable oil with him to lubricate squeaky hinges. False floorboards were another trick, some boards having been specially prepared so that the slightest pressure emitted a loud noise. To avoid this the ninja employed a special series of walking techniques, which he had learned all those years before when training on wet rice paper.

Once inside the chamber the ninja held the sleeping lord at his mercy. Death could come in an instant by a quick flash of a blade. But because the rich nobles went so much in fear for their lives, it was not unusual for them to be checked by their Samurai guards every hour of the day and night. If a noble was discovered murdered, a hue and cry would follow and thus reduce the ninja's chances down of effecting a swift and safe escape. So for his own security the ninja would probably despatch the sleeping lord using a slow-acting poison, which he always carried with him.

The Invisible Warrior

Master of poisons

Being a master of all types of poison, especially herbal concoctions, the ninja knew every plant and shrub in the forest, including those containing the deadliest poisons. Some potions were used to paralyse, others as hallucinogens. To a superstitious Samurai, another Samurai with the effects of a hallucinogen in their system would appear to be possessed of evil spirits and demons. The ninja's knowledge of chemistry and botany can be equated with that of a pharmacist. He may not have had access to the sophisticated poisons or drugs of today, but the organic mixtures he used were just as deadly.

One particular favourite the ninja found regular use for was the poison from the *fugu* (blowfish). In Japan even today this fish is considered a special delicacy, and at certain fugu-licensed restaurants one can enjoy this dish. This fish is so deadly poisonous, the active ingredient called tetradoxin being in its every organ, that the Japanese government issue cooks with a special licence to prepare it.

Fugu poison carried around in a special container could be rubbed upon the lips of the sleeping lord. The poison attacks the respiratory system, paralysing the muscles related to breathing. The ninja, having fulfilled his mission, then had ample time to leave the castle without the alarm being raised at the death of the lord. When morning came the quick-acting poison, the effects of which had been slowed down by being applied only to the lips, suddenly reacted and the ninja's mission was complete. Yet although he had left the castle earlier, he did not leave the vicinity until he knew his mission was a success.

Making good his escape

The mission completed, the ninja would set off on the long journey back to the clan encampment. He knew that all the border guards would have been alerted and search parties would be out hunting him. The ninja's expertise in surviving outdoors against the elements, and also against all odds, was legendary. Through his early extensive training he could exist alone in the wilds on a day-to-day basis. Sometimes if an escape route was blocked, the ninja would have to travel many miles out of his way in order to be free. The rations he would have originally taken with him for the job would probably have run out and to get home he would have to live off the land.

The woods and fields were the ninja's kitchen. The Japanese *daikon* (giant radish) grew in abundance so he could sustain himself with this. A substance made from soya beans called *tofu* was easily digested and rich in protein and the ninja often carried this on his person as an emergency ration. As an expert in nutrition the ninja was wary of heavy foods such as greasy or oily meals which take a long time to digest and have the effect of making the body sluggish, giving a feeling of lethargy and consequently slowing him down. A balanced diet was essential if he were to survive out in the wilds. Thus it wasn't just a matter of the ninja eating anything that was available: he had to be particular.

Often while escaping the ninja agent could fall foul of a skirmish with the enemy and become injured. If he was wounded or ill in any way, with no doctor at hand, he could possibly die. In this situation his knowledge of pharmacy was vital. He knew of certain types of mushrooms growing in the forest, such as the puffball fungi, which would cure infected wounds. The puffball emits a dust when squeezed that is rich in an antibiotic not unlike penicillin. A sword cut quickly healed when this forest medicine was applied.

Constantly wary of pursuit the ninja avoided all signs of civilization, keeping only to the desolate and secluded areas for fear of being seen. In an alien environment the ninja kept a constant look-out for the tell-tale signs of habitated areas. As an expert tracker he knew that ruts on the pathways meant that farmers had pulled their carts along here and so this was a route to be avoided. Spirals of smoke through the trees told him that a hut or house was near by. If he was completely lost in an area that was totally new to him, the ninja would look around for a felled tree or even fell a small one himself just so that he could examine the rings on the tree stump. This he knew acted as an excellent direction finder since the rings always grow biggest and peak in the direction of the south. The ninja warrior was never at a loss for keeping himself alive by one means or another. When a ninja was thirsty and could not get to water for fear of being discovered, he would suck a type of lozenge made from peppermint powder which would slake his thirst until water was found. Yet a ninja's sense of awareness was honed to razor sharpness to such an extent it is said that like an animal he could smell water from a great distance.

Killing the pursuing enemy

Once his pursuers were perhaps gaining on him the ninja would examine what options were open to him. He could maybe try to out-run them, but if they were mounted Samurai this could prove a little difficult. Faced with such a predicament the ninja would enter a dense part of the forest and set about arranging a series of booby-traps. In the dark depths of the forest the ninja was on home ground. All his lifetime's experience came to the fore as he thought up devastating traps to ensnare and kill his pursuing enemy.

The Invisible Warrior

Stakes with sharpened ends tipped with animal dung would be concealed in the dense undergrowth and these had the effect of poisoning the bloodstream. Small gullies would be dug out and covered with leaves so that the pursuers horses would trip, breaking their legs. Sapling trees would be bent back and secured with vines on a hidden trip wire running across a pathway. Once this wire was disturbed the sapling would fly out and whack the horsemen off their mounts. A myriad of devices was available to the ingenious ninja warrior, for in the half-light and shadows of the forest, the pursuers were in his domain and often at his mercy.

If no forests were near, and his pursuers were homing in fast, the ninja would simply hide by using his special techniques of self-camouflage. This entailed the ninja blending in with his surroundings at any given moment. He would dash behind a tree stump or a rock and become part of that object. Because of the subtle training methods he had studied as a child he was able to concentrate his mind and focus it towards melting into his surroundings. Once in that state he could shape his body to correspond to his environment. He would curl up into a ball and look just like another stone or boulder, which would prove very confusing to his pursuers looking for telltale arms and legs. By wrapping himself around the trunk of a tree, the ninja assumed the pose of a tree and became part of it. This ability to remain motionless for extended periods of time ensured his pursuers would simply ride right past him without noticing.

The ninja with three wives

The great pains to which a ninja went in order to remain free have been the source of many legends. History has recorded that a famous ninja named Sandayu Momochi, who was a founder of the Iga ninja, maintained three different homes, each with a wife and family. In each of these homes he adopted a different lifestyle. For instance, in one city he would be a merchant, in another he was lamp maker, and the third saw him as a farmer. In creating this situation for himself his anonymity was assured. He could operate in one area and if discovery seemed likely he would disappear and emerge 50 miles away as another person complete with wife and family

This ruse was so successful that in 1581 when the ninja-hater Lord Oda Nobunaga sent out his 46,000 troops against the ninja clans, Sandayu escaped and assumed one of his alternative identities. He kept these tricks up all his life and was never captured. Sandayu had many students in his lifetime, but his greatest was a man called Goemon Ishikawa, who has been called the bandit hero of Japan and is often likened to Robin Hood. Unfortunately for this unlikely hero neither the Iga nor Koga ninja would acknowledge him as their own, because he used his ninja skills for personal gain rather than for the benefit of the clans.

Perhaps the most famous of all was Hanzo Hattori who ended his days in the service of the great Shogun Ieyasu. In one of the many tales that surround his escapades, Hattori is said to have built a type of paddle-boat with a huge saw on the bow. This boat was used to destroy the early wooden submarines that had been sent against his Shogun by rival ninja factions.

Merciless torture

Even after long years of training, the ninja agents were deemed expendable by the hierarchy of chunin and jonin. So it was therefore in the ninja's own hands whether or not he survived on a mission. Occasionally a ninja agent was caught while executing his mission. He knew that if this happened he would be tortured mercilessly and put to death very slowly, his captors doing everything in their power to make him talk before he died. The ninja clans had an iron-clad law or code of discipline that forbade divulging information. The ninja was sworn to secrecy about his training, his contacts, and of course the whereabouts of the main ninja encampment. Thus the ninja chose death (often by his own hand) rather than betray his fellow warriors. Any ninja who was disloyal was ruthlessly hunted down by other members of the clan and put to death. So strong was this code of honour, that if a small group of ninja was operating in an area and it looked as though one of them might be caught, he would be killed instantly by his own associates before they made good their own escape.

Finally the ninja agent, after completing his mission and evading his pursuers, arrived back at his own encampment. The fees for the assassination or information gathering would be paid to the jonin. As for the field agent himself, his only reward was the knowledge of a job well done and to be welcomed back into the fold of the ninja clan family unit, to be fed and clothed, sheltered and warmed – until the next mission.

Living in the West it is perhaps hard to imagine surviving under such austere conditions. But we must not forget that from birth this is the only world and life the ninja had known. It has been suggested that in the latter days of ninjutsu activity many of the *genin* (ordinary agents) were not as accomplished as their forebears. This could have been from the constant interbreeding – a result of their isolation – which produced genetic defects and lead to some clans becoming almost extinct.

The Invisible Warrior

One good plan is worth a thousand men

Although his combat skills were of supreme importance, the ninja's most lethal weapon was his own mind. Trained from birth to observe anything and everything within man and nature the ninja was at one with himself and his environment. His thought process and logical application were far superior to even the Samurai war chiefs who had benefited from a classical and military education. Before a ninja set out on a mission he looked at every aspect of what the job entailed and the chances of its successful completion. By applying the mind the ninja tried to allow for every consequence. It is said that even fate cannot prevent the 'unknown quantity', the X factor of the unknown. But because of their tried and tested methods of adapting to all manner of situations the ninja could usually rely upon themselves to get out of a sticky situation by bluff and subterfuge.

Having arrived at the intended destination the ninja would do nothing except observe and then observe again, ensuring that every possible and conceivable calculation had been taken into account. These calculations would include the terrain and the immediate tactical situation. By waiting and preparing the ninja could assess what needed to be done so that he wouldn't be seen and yet still gather the information required.

Secret Art of the Ninja

It is said one good plan is worth a thousand men, so tactics and strategy and the skilful use of both were always foremost in the ninja's mind. Sometimes a ninja sent to observe a hostile force purely on a reconnaissance mission took it upon himself to kill two birds with one stone. If the opportunity arose whereby the leader or Samurai chief of the enemy force breached his own security by being alone, even if just for an instant, the ninja observer would act upon his own initiative and strike the man dead. Quietly and unobserved he would probably slit the throat of the Samurai chief and escape, reporting to his immediate superior what he had done. A leaderless army is a demoralized army and the officers often took the army home. This is best exemplified by the old oriental proverb, 'The river that can drown an elephant can be stopped at its source with a twig.'

The ninja, unlike most feudal and medieval fighting forces anywhere in the world, were years ahead of their time in terms of military accomplishments using terrorist or guerrilla warfare tactics. Today, almost every country in the world has a Special Forces unit operating within the army, navy and airforce. These units are home to a kind of super soldier with advanced skills far in excess of normal military training. But the ninja in Japan 500 years ago was comparable to and also the forerunner of any elite group or fighting force in operation today. Considering the military development of the period and the strict chain of command in most armies of the time, the ninja thought for themselves and often acted far in excess of orders. This ensured they were equally formidable alone as in a group. Their mentality epitomised Sun Tsu's comment of, 'He is truly wise who knows when to fight and when not to fight'.

The rise of the ninja

I have spoken previously about the political climate in which the ninja were able to flouish. To understand fully how the clans managed to survive for as many as 600 years it is equally important to fully understand this climate.

During the Heian period (AD 794–1192) Japan's social scale rose to so called civilized society. The three social classes at the time were the Lords or Daimyos, the Warrior class (the Samurai) and the ordinary peasant class which comprised about 80 per cent of the population. The artisans and merchants within Japanese society were looked down upon. During the course of these three centuries, some great and powerful families emerged in Japan. These were termed as clans. These families, the biggest and most notable being the Taira, Minamoto, and Sugawara, vied and fought and schemed constantly in an effort to become the most powerful in the land.

The heads of these families each sought to fight their enemies and claim land and belongings to add to their already growing wealth. But constantly fighting wars with one's neighbours is a costly experience. So short cuts were sought in this neverending almost feud-like existence.

One obvious short cut was to hire, at far less cost, the services of mercenaries or assassins who would strike down the opposing leader or commander, leaving the lords free to simply walk in and claim the land and castles for themselves. The ninja thus came into their own, and money was forever exchanging hands to bring about the demise of first one lord and then another. This tit for tat murder complex saw the eventual decimation of many great families. As for the ninja they just got richer and richer and more powerful.

By the end of the Heian period the family or clan of the Fujiwara had come to prominence. To preserve law and order in the capital Kyoto, this clan found it increasingly useful to call upon the mercenary forces of the so-called military clans (armies of other lords and landowners). However, by enlisting the support of these other families to fight their battles for them, the Fujiwara who were mainly hedonistic and political found themselves suddenly on the outside with all their power wrested from them and in the hands of the very people they had hired to protect them.

The Invisible Warrior

The Taira clan were the first to usurp the Fujiwara and lay claim to the imperial court and government. Under their family head Kiyomori Taira, they held a 25 year administration during which they used guile, intermarriage, assassination and political intrigue to forge a cast iron grip on the central government. But a short time after his death in 1181 his heirs, grown soft through court life, were suddenly met with an overwhelming force from another military family, the Minamoto. After seizing power from the Taira they took the power of administration and government away from Kyoto and established a new powerbase in the city of Kamakura.

The Taira hired mercenaries and a final showdown took place at a great sea battle in the Shimonoseki Straits in 1185 which is south-west of where modern day Tokyo stands. The Taira were utterly vanquished, and Yorimoto Monamoto set up a system of government in Kamakura known as the *Bakufu*, which literally means camp office. And the Emperor of Japan, a boy barely in his teens, bestowed upon Yorimoto the title of Sei-tai-Shogun which means *Barbarian subduing Generalissimo*. Thus the so-called Kamakura period, which was to last for 150 years, was ushered in. This was also the first time the population of Japan truly knew that the government was now permanently in the hands of the military class.

The Kamakura period is remembered in Japanese

history not only for the consolidation of the power of the military houses but also for great tales of heroism and the romantic age of chivalry. Religion and the arts flourished but also envy and greed within other military families.

The rise of the Samurai with their *Bushido* (code of ethics) and as an elite military class was also seen. It is difficult to draw comparisons between what was happening in Japan during this period and its counterparts in the Western world. Perhaps the best comparison to make would be with the Roman Empire type of government minus the senate.

With so much in-fighting and struggles for power and position at this time in Japan, it is not difficult to see how the ninja clans rose to such significance and that the type of trade they practised was much sought after.

The Bakufu government eventually passed into the hands of the Hojo family who ruled for a time but the inevitable intrigues and political plotting led to the emergence of Takauji Ashikaga of the house of Minamoto. He set himself up as Shogun and moved the centre of government back to Kyoto, in the area known as Muromachi. This Ashikaga Shogunate, as it was known, lasted nearly 250 years. During that time the ninja never had it so good. The conditions of the period were so chaotic, marred by continuous violence, full-scale civil wars and total breakdowns of law and order, with most Daimyos becoming almost a law unto themselves. An air of paranoia existed between all the leaders of the military houses, who often quite saturated themselves with bodyguards of Samuari to protect them from their enemies' assassins. The ninja plied their trade with deadly efficiency, working for whoever could pay them the most. Quite often one lord would pay the ninja for a series of assassinations, only to be killed himself some months later by the same ninja clan, paid by the relatives of the dead lord in retribution.

It is hard to imagine the sheer scale of devastation during this period of Japanese history. And yet at the same time the mighty Shogun, nestled in his great castle, lived an insular life impervious to everything that was going on within the country. In a way, an almost strange paradox existed, because it was during this age that the religion of Zen Buddhism developed, especially within the ranks of the Samurai and the arts of painting and the skills of the swordsmiths were perfected.

New technology

When the first Portuguese sailors and traders arrived on the shores of Japan from China in 1542, with the *arquebus*, the smooth bore early musket. This the Japanese soon learned to manufacture on their own and the new art of the gunsmith began to rival that of even the ancient skills of the swordsmith. For the ninja, a new epoch had opened, the device for killing at a distance.

Taking the technology of the musket further the ninja began to experiment in packing gourds tightly with a mixture of gunpowder and musket balls, with a small fuse protruding out of the end. The gourd could then be tossed into a group of soldiers or mounted horsemen and the resulting explosion would send a cluster of deadly lead balls flying in all directions. This killed the enemy faster and in larger numbers than any arrow could, causing distraction and confusion at the same time.

Money had replaced the old peasant currency of paying for everything with rice. So the ninja middle-men eagerly approached these Portuguese traders and paid in gold for their deadly cargoes.

Deadly Weapons

A single false move loses the game.

THE ninja and their art of ninjutsu employed a vast collection of weird and wonderful weapons. If ever a man could be termed a walking arsenal, it would certainly be the ninja warrior. On his missions he carried an awesome array of weapons and gadgets that would aid him in defeating an enemy. Because the ninja's missions often took him hundreds of miles away from his own area, and he would not know what facilities were available to him at his destination, he had to carry everything he needed on his person. All the ninja's weapons were of a very distinctive nature. Many had dual purposes to cut down on travelling weight. They had to be extremely effective yet light, and concealable enough to be carried inside the ninja's *shinobishozuki* (uniform). To carry a back pack or rucksack of some description would have meant bringing attention to himself and therefore raise questions. So unless the job was of a particular specialist nature the ninja went off into the night with both hands free.

The ninja sword

Perhaps the most readily identifiable weapon of the ninja was his *shinobikatana* (sword). The ninja sword was totally different from the Samurai's beloved weapon. It was generally short (about 20 inches/50 cm in length), having a single-edged straight blade with an oversized *tsuba* (handguard). Because the blade was short the ninja would strap it to his back and thus keep his hands free. If he were suddenly attacked the sword could be unsheathed while still on his back and put quickly into action. The low ceilings in Japanese houses prohibited a very long sword being drawn in this manner, but a short, straight 20-inch blade proved to be no problem. The ninja's sword was a veritable box of tricks. The scabbard was longer than the blade by about 3 inches (7.5cm). This extra space allowed the ninja to store poisons, powdered medicines and flash powders in its detachable bottom. If he was pursued by enemy soldiers he could remove this lower piece of the scabbard, dive into a river or lake and use the hollow scabbard to breath through. Over and over again, tricks such as these not only confused the enemy but laid the foundation for the ninja being thought of as superhuman spirits that could disappear at will. The long cord used for strapping on the sword could be put to a multitude of uses, for instance as a rope to tie up a prisoner or in conjunction with the extra large hand-guard for helping the ninja over some high obstacle such as a castle wall.

In the forest he could snare small game using the cord as a slip-knot noose. The sword had a very different meaning for the ninja than it did for the Samurai. The Samurai carried two swords which, along with his top-knotted hair, was the mark of a warrior. His trusty *katana* (swords) were made from high-grade carbon steel and each took skilled swordsmiths months to make as they hammered and folded and hammered again the edge of the blade until it contained hundreds of layers of finely forged steel. The reverence a Samurai gave such a weapon was little short of worship. His blade was his very being, his honour, his code, even his soul. The ninja's sword, on the other hand, had a blade that was of very poor quality and dull in comparison to the razor-sharp edge of the Samurai's. It resembled nothing more than a short piece of sharpened iron with a handle and was crudely forged using less than ideal materials. The finished product often had a tendency to break. To the ninja, his sword was just another tool of the trade.

A hundred and one weapons

If a ninja was confronted out in the open by a Samurai he was at an immediate disadvantage if he had to rely on his sword alone. But the ninja had plenty of other nefarious little weapons concealed about his person to more than even up the odds. When a ninja did use his short sword to fight with, he employed the scabbard as well, which could be used for blocking and countering. Throughout his childhood training the ninja would have been taught to master a hundred and one different types of weapons. Bo staffs, sticks and canes were all regarded as important weapons. An ordinary bo staff (6 foot/1.8m-pole) in the hands of a ninja disguised as a wandering Buddhist priest could suddenly be revealed as a devastating arsenal of hidden weapons. Before the startled adversary could react, the priest-cum-ninja, with a quick flick of the wrist, could propel a small sharp missile into the chest of his enemy from the hollowed out bo staff which was spring loaded. The versatile bo staff could even be converted into a one-shot musket. If a Samurai advanced upon a cornered ninja, the bo staff end was flicked off and out would come a lethal swirling

Deadly Weapons

chain with which the ninja could ensnare his enemy, then move in close and finish him off with his short black *tanto* (dagger). Quite often when confronting a ninja, enemy soldiers preferred not to face him man to man but tried to finish him off with a bow and arrow, or by hurling a spear at him.

Chains and cords of death

Another favoured fighting instrument of the ninja was the *kusarigama*, which was a long-range blade and chain weapon. A ninja could hurl the chain with its weighted end at an enemy from a safe distance, entangle him and then move in close with the sickle-shaped blade and cut him to pieces. A similar weapon to that of the kusarigama, but used much earlier in ninja history, was the *kyoketsu shoge*. This had a hook blade with an 18-foot-long (5.5m) length of cord attached to it, with an iron ring fastened on to the opposite end. It was used exclusively by the ninja, and here again the long cord could be put to use in a hundred other ways when not being used as a weapon. Another ninja weapon in the same vein was called a *kusarifundo* or 'ten thousand power chain'. This consisted of a short length of chain about 20 inches (50cm) long with two heavy metal weights attached to each end. The kusarifundo was easily concealed in the ninja's uniform pocket and could be produced in an instant. One end of the chain was held in the hand and the weight at the other end was hurled outwards in a similar manner to that of a child's yo-yo. The heavy metal ball would hit the adversary and stun him, the ninja then would quickly move

Ninja chain weapons which include the *manrikusari*, *kusarigama* and *kusarifundo*. These weapons, which are easily concealed inside the ninja's tunic, could be produced in an instant.

Deadly Weapons

in and close the distance to finish the enemy off with a strangulation technique using the chain. Although a short-range weapon the kusarifundo was extremely effective in a tight situation.

Sowing poisonous seeds

The ninja uniform, the shinobishozuki, consisted of jacket, trousers, hood, and special shoes called *tabi* which were split-toed. Within this garb were many concealed pockets and pouches in which the ninja carried all manner of useful items to aid him on his mission. Each of the ninja clans had their own distinctive versions of common weapons. Many of these wouldn't have even been considered a weapon by the ordinary footsoldier or Samurai. But to the ninja they could mean the difference between escape and capture. The *tetsubishi* or caltrop was a small escape and evasion weapon used exclusively by the ninja. This weapon carried a barb similar to those seen on barbed wire and it could be scattered around a ninja's route of escape, so that when his pursuers gave chase they would tread on the sharp points and fall down in pain. Because the ninja often coated these tetsubishi with poison, a pursuing enemy not only fell down in agony but stark fear entered their hearts at the thought of not knowing whether what they had just stepped upon was poisonous or not. Usually this was enough to halt any pursuer from further chasing the ninja.

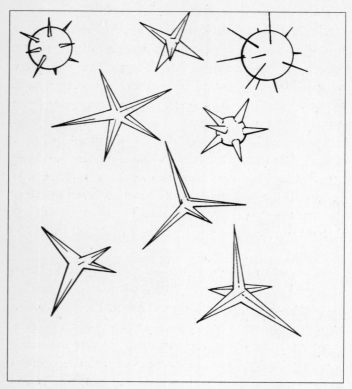

Ninja caltrops or *tetsubishi:* sharp metal spikes tipped with poison that would be strewn in the path of a pursuing enemy.

Deadly Weapons

Using forward planning the ninja could enter a castle and leave tetsubishi scattered around a small passageway, which would serve to slow down any pursuer. If the ninja had to jump out of a second-storey window he would, upon landing, let the enemy see him scattering the caltrops. This effectively stopped them following him down, and they would have to give chase from another direction. Should the ninja have cause to scale a wall to make good his escape, once he was over the top he would place a series of caltrops along the wall. A pursuer vaulting up after him would suddenly find his hands impaled on the deadly spikes. Even in hand-to-hand combat, the tetsubishi were thrown into the enemy's face to distract him long enough for the ninja to close in for the kill.

It is perhaps interesting to note that the Daimyo cottoned on to the use of caltrops as a security device and they were often scattered around the hallways at night to prevent unwelcome visitors from suddenly bursting in. As always the ninja was prepared even for this eventuality. Once he had discovered the caltrops in the vicinity, his special methods of walking allowed him gently to push them in front of him with the side of his foot. Making no noise he would sweep them along, gaining entrance to the particular room he required and carrying out the deed. In his escape he left the caltrops in their new position, a pursuing enemy then being confronted by his own strewn devices and having no way of knowing if they were the original castle weapons or if the ninja had strewn them – in which case the tips could be poisoned. Because tetsubishi were used in such large numbers it would be impossible for the ninja to carry a large supply on his person. So therefore when he ran out, nature lent a hand. The ninja would go into the forest and gather water chestnut shells, which have a similar shape to the tetsubishi. These would then be coated with either animal dung or a poison from his own pocket

Climbing like a cat

A very prominent ninja weapon that had a dual role was the *shuko*. This implement, which was worn on the hands like a pair of gloves, allowed the ninja to grip very smooth and hard surfaces. It was primarily used for scaling a castle wall to gain entry into his intended victim's chambers. The shuko, also known as *tekagi*, was made of one narrow and one wide metal band joined by a flat metal section. The narrow band slipped over the hand and tightened around the wrist, leaving the wide band to encircle the hand. Four sharp spikes protruded from the palm of the wide band. Apart from these climbing claws giving the ninja access to difficult places and the climbing

Deadly Weapons

abilities of a cat, they could be used for close-quarter fighting. If suddenly surprised by a sword-wielding guard on the castle battlements, the ninja could easily block a sword strike to his head by using the shuko. In retaliation the ninja could then strike out using the spikes to injure the guard and make good his escape.

Shuriken – the star-shaped missile

Perhaps the most famous weapon of the ninja was the shuriken, the star-shaped missile that could be thrown with deadly accuracy. Although multi-pointed shuriken were the type most commonly used, the various ninja clans used other shapes as well, such as the swastika, originally a Sanskrit emblem. Other shuriken resembled short darts or knife blades. Shuriken were easily concealed in a pocket, but within easy reach if they were needed in an emergency. Because of the mystical overtones in the ninja clans, most field agents carried nine shuriken in their pocket, this number being considered lucky.

During childhood training the ninja would have repeatedly thrown the shuriken into targets shaped as humans until his accuracy was assured. Aim and timing became almost second nature, and a ninja could throw shuriken so fast that it was not unusual actually to have six or seven in the air at the same time. The shuriken is held between the thumb and the forefinger, and thrown in a similar method to that of dealing out cards. The razor-sharp pointed objects whizzing through the air would throw even the hardiest of pursuers into a panic. Again the tips of these shuriken would no doubt have been coated with some form of poison, so the slightest scratch could mean certain death. The ninja, if disturbed while wandering through the darkened chambers of a sleeping castle, could spread panic and confusion by hurling the star-shaped objects into the room. Because shuriken were black they would be virtually invisible to the naked eye if hurled into a darkened room. A ninja would always retain at least one shuriken upon his person for close-quarter combat. An enemy struggling with a cornered ninja could suddenly find a very sharp shuriken placed under his armpit and his arm forced downwards onto the evil points.

When the ninja threw the shuriken he would stack them up in his hand and hurl them one after another at an oncoming enemy. They would slide out of the hand in a rapid flicking movement and cut through the air with power and accuracy to find their target in the throat or face of an enemy pursuer. The straight bladed shuriken could be held in a bunch and thrown at an enemy one at a time as if throwing darts. Skilled Shuriken throwing lies in utilizing the wrist and fingers in such a manner that tension is

Deadly Weapons

added at the moment of release. The body is angled so that it is behind the motion of the throw. A stiff and rigid stance when throwing the deadly blades inhibits the aim and distance. Balance and body harmony act as one to ensure a proper delivery and achieve the required effect.

Arrows from nowhere

The *yumi* was the ninja bow and arrow, which was carried about in a bamboo tube for protection. This ninja weapon was much shorter than the conventional longbow of the Samurai and Japanese troops, which facilitated its easy transportation. The ninja could ambush his designated target with ease from some concealed position. An arrow flying out of nowhere could not be heard or seen – just felt. His aim and accuracy was such that he usually only needed one arrow to accomplish his task.

A lord out hunting with his retainers would suddenly fall from his mount mortally wounded. The hapless Samurai could search all day long for the perpetrator, but to no avail. The lone ninja appeared as a ghost in the forest and melted back just as easily, his task accomplished. More than likely the ninja would have burrowed under the earth and then covered himself over with a type of trap door. A small spy hole would have enabled him to see his target approach.

Secret Art of the Ninja

Earlier, the ninja most probably spent days taking notes of his target's daily habits, thus establishing a routine. As time was of no consequence to the ninja – only the mission mattered – he could take note of every detail and thus arrange an ambush that had everything in his own favour in terms of conceal-ment and escape.

The ninja's ingenuity for adaptation enabled him to make all types of arrows and so create havoc inside enemy positions. Specially constructed arrows car-ried messages, bombs, flares, and even ropes so that difficult walls or cliffs could be scaled easily. Sometimes the ninja tipped the point of his arrow with poison, thus making sure that the enemy would die even if he were initially only slightly wounded. An invading army could soon be put to rout by using a few well-placed ninja with fire and exploding arrows.

Over the many years as technology grew so did the ninja's arsenal. With explosives came the ninja's own homemade mortar. Exploding land-mines, although crudely constructed, were often very effec-tive. Other weapons they carried and used were flutes, which could be converted into blowpipes for poisonous darts. The *yari* or common spear was adapted to become the *bisento*, a type of wide-bladed spear.

Deadly Weapons

Walking on water

When looking at the ninja's tools of the trade, weapons constituting just a small part of this category, one cannot help being in awe at the lengths he went to in order to be successful. Legends relate that the ninja could walk on water just like a *kami* spirit. In fact, this is only part truth. The ninja was able to ford a river, but only by means of a water-crossing device called a *ukidaru* or floating pot. These were water-proof reed pots which the ninja wore on each leg like a huge pair of waders. Aided by a long bamboo pole the ninja could cross a castle moat or river with relative ease and in this way could keep his explosive powders dry. The ninja's prowess at swimming great distances and holding his breath underwater for long periods of time has already been described. Thus to the frightened peasants the superstition that ninja could assume the powers of fish and live underwater seemed perfectly reasonable. For a feudal Japanese farmer, witnessing an escaping ninja dive into a lake or river and not come back up until after the pursuing troops had returned home, was enough to make his blood run cold.

Travelling light

Quite often the ninja's mission involved the penetration of enemy lines and fortifications for purposes of assassination or espionage. Such missions required stealth, speed and unencumbered manoeuvrability. This being the case, the ninja often travelled lightly armed. If he was discovered by a Samurai warrior, or rival ninja, he would turn his attacker's weapon back upon him, killing his assailant and then retaining the weapon for his own use. Finally, one of the most practical weapons the ninja used which was always on hand was a short stick about 3 feet (1m) in length called a hanbo or half-staff. This stick could be used for striking, throwing and locking techniques.

The environment as a weapon

Apart from the known weapons of the time, the ninja also used his environment as a tool in self defence. Trailing vines could be used for strangulations, smooth pebbles thrown with great force could take the place of a shuriken. In fact, if the ninja was cornered in the forest or on a mountain top anything and everything around him could be utilized, limited only by the powers of his own imagination. The woods and mountains were his home and no matter where the ninja travelled on a mission he would never be at a loss for some form of weapon to defend himself. As for his enemy, the Samurai and footsoldiers, once out of the safety of the castle and their familiar environs, it was they who were at a disadvantage.

Deadly Weapons

Adaptable weapons

Weapons and the development of weapons technology, however primitive in those times, was of great importance to the ninja. To maintain an edge over the enemy anything new was examined in great detail in order to ascertain its use in the field. Adaptable weapons which served more than one purpose were an even greater advantage. As we have seen in the previous chapter the introduction of the gun in the 16th century gave added impetus to the ninja's steadily growing arsenal of weapons.

The Ninja Way of Life

*To learn the true meaning
of victory, go and ask the
defeated warrior*

THE art of ninjutsu employs a vast collection of esoteric knowledge that provides the basis for the ninja's
unique approach to life and the understanding of it.
They, more than any, were at one with their environment. Ninja and the art they so fervently follow is a
total way of life in which all aspects of nature and the
natural elements, plus man's own consciousness and
total perspective of his understanding, are blended
together, to provide a life that is at one and in harmony
with the universe.

The five elemental manifestations

The Shugendo teachings of the ninja were heavily
influenced by many of the East's mystical doctrines,

incorporating into their realm such treatises as the Tao Te Ching, I Ching, and the Tantric beliefs of Tibet, plus of course Buddhism. These, and other forms of mysticism, were used in experiencing and interpreting the will and flow of the universe. Ninjutsu tactics and techniques often take on board the symbolism of nature to provide inspiration for practical application. Within the philosophy of ninjutsu are incorporated what are known as the Go Dai, the five elemental manifestations. These are: Ku=Void, Fu=Wind, Ka=Fire, Sui=Water, Chi=Earth.

This progression depicts the creation of the universe and symbolizes the ways that physical matter manifests itself as formless combustive energy creating in its turn energy liquids, solids and gas. From this come what are termed the Go Gyo, or five prime elements which describe how things interrelate and operate, much like the Chinese yin and yang. These elements are: Chi=Earth, Sui=Water, Ka=Fire, Moku=Wood, Kin=Metal. Continuously working, these elements interact to create and then destroy each other. Water feeds the growing tree, which is then felled by the metal axe, and then consumed by the fire to finally scatter into ashes on the earth. The ninja align these five principles so that they can be seen as they operate in the regulation of an individual's health and also in the unfolding of life's events.

The ninja's Taoist heritage, taken from Chinese

teachings over a thousand years before, brought about a familiarity with nature, and natural laws became the theory behind the application of ninjutsu escape skills. The skill of *tonjutsu*, the earth methods, involved the use of rocks, soil and land contours to aid the ninja in his escape. *Sui tonjutsu*, or water methods, involve the use of special equipment for moving across the surface of ponds, rivers, swamps, moats and lakes, as well as utilizing unique techniques and apparatus for remaining submerged under water for long periods.

Invoking the kuji power principle

One of the most misunderstood aspects of ninjutsu by non-practitioners of the art is the ninja concept of *kuji*. Kuji means 'nine syllables' and it is one of the most exotic and to some, bizarre skills of the ancient ninja warriors. By weaving their fingers together in what resembled something of a Gordian knot, and at the same time mumbling an obscure incantation, the ninja could perform the most impossible task that would make mere mortals cringe. Legends relate that the ninja walked across water, disappeared like ghosts, flew through the air like demons, and were invisible to humans. The truth behind these stories arises from ninja applying the kuji principles of mind and body in total harmony and their ability to adapt to any given situation. In reality, the kuji power principle stems from the ancient mystical teachings of northern India and Tibet. These were brought to Japan during China's T'ang dynasty (AD 618-907) and formed part of the esoteric lore that later came to be known as Mikkyo or the secret doctrines.

Today's ninja practitioners and students, after adopting the standard ninja training syllabus, go on to learn the higher order of the ninja art which they term *Ninpo*. Ninpo reflects the nature of the art and the needs that caused it to come into being. The kuji hand-weaving configurations are, in actuality, only one-third of the whole of the kuji concept. They represent the physical body in action, which must then be joined by the intellect and the will in order to produce the desired results.

The three elements of thought, word and deed, are co-ordinated and attuned with each other to make up the ninja's kuji power principle. This system is, in reality, a method of learning to remove the gap that separates intention from successful action. The rational mind, having its own limitations, can refuse subconsciously to attempt anything that seems impossible. But by overriding this natural process anything and everything becomes possible to the ninja, who at the same time still retains the feasibility choice. Or in other words by invoking the kuji power principle, the user begins not only to believe he can apply himself towards an endeavour, but also knows that it will be a success without endangering himself. Once the kuji technique is mastered the ninja then has the power to create physical reality by means of his intention alone. Focused intention becomes completed action itself: cause blends with effect until the distinction fades.

The mind as a weapon

Invoking kuji power in a combat application allows the ninja the ability to focus his intention to gain power or energy that seems to defy normal physical laws. This intention-focusing does not actually create extra energy, but rather removes the limits that usually restrict the amount of energy available to the normal individual. This concept is similar to the adepts of yoga, who by focusing their mind and will are able to perform seemingly extraordinary feats that defy explanation. Advanced mystical techniques such as this gave the illusion to the uninitiated that the invoker possessed great magical power, and where ignorance abounds, legends begin.

A common misconception about this higher order of the art is that ninjutsu followers put themselves in danger by adopting the kuji methods of trance-like action. This is totally wrong. The physical body is capable of performing the techniques; the mind understands what has to be done; and the will is unhesitating and determines that the task will be completed successfully.

The mind as a weapon can be truly awesome if applied to the right area of circumstances. None knew this better than the ninja himself: basic and advanced psychology were important lessons that the ninja learned thoroughly if he was to stay alive. Every advantage was an edge. The ninja saw the average person as having five basic weaknesses, which he categorized as Fear, Sympathy, Vanity, Anger and Laziness. He found the greatest weapon was exploiting one of these weaknesses. Some adversaries almost always react in the same manner and can be identified with one specific weakness above all others, but others fluctuate from one weakness to another, depending on the circumstances. By capitalizing on an adversary's emotional weakness, the ninja could manipulate his target's fundamental needs.

In an espionage manoeuvre a ninja agent, by catering to or supplying a need, could develop a feeling of obligation in the person being cultivated. Later, this debt could be touched upon when the ninja needed assistance or some item of information. Again the ninja classified these basic needs into five broad categories: Security, Sex, Wealth, Pride and Pleasure.

Ninja mind games

The ninja agent, also a mere mortal, could fall into his own trap of self-desires. If a need arose within the ninja's own personality, such as pride, pleasure or even wealth – the weaknesses he was taught to look out for in others – then he could be caught in the 'needs' trap. The ninja's key to overcoming this problem in his mental make-up was for him mentally to run through a kind of self-examination programme. In this mind game, he examined his own needs and wants, and then openly and honestly evaluated them, judged them for what they were and then cast them aside. In knowing himself, the ninja could come to an honest appraisal of his weaknesses and those areas where he was vulnerable. After reaching this point, the ninja would then find ways of strengthening the potential trouble areas in his own egotistical make-up. The ninja agent could not allow any kind of self-weakness to mar his thinking and thus make him weak. He could not just close his eyes and pretend the weakness did not exist. Ultimately he had to satisfy his needs through personal understanding, and eventually work the weaknesses out of his personality.

This brilliant ability for self-analysis could take him to the stage where he could totally overcome most basic inherent human traits, to arrive at the position where he could actually conquer the ego itself.

Secret Art of the Ninja

Incredible as it may sound, the ninja's mental ability was such that he could be put on a par with today's practising psychologists. This inestimable power of catering to a person's inner wants and needs gave the ninja a very powerful weapon indeed. The kunoichi perhaps excelled in these abilities more so than their male counterparts.

The fearless ones

A famous ninja escapade involved the ninja folk hero Goemon. In fact, the plot of this legend is so fascinating that hundreds of years later it was used for a sequence in the James Bond movie *You Only Live Twice*. The story relates that Goemon was sent to kill the notorious Oda Nobunaga. After great difficulties in gaining entrance to his castle (it is said Goemon waited over two months in the area) he finally succeeded in entering and quickly made his way to Nobunaga's sleeping quarters, which to his dismay were completely surrounded by his Samurai bodyguards. Using his imaginative powers, Goemon crawled along the precarious rafters above the ceiling and entered a small attic above the lord's bedchamber. Next he drilled a small hole into the ceiling right in line with Nobunaga's *futon* (bed). When the lord retired for the night, Goemon waited until the man was fast asleep. Then noiselessly he lowered a thin silk strand until it hung suspended just above the lips of his sleeping victim. Taking out a small phial of deadly poison from his concealed pouch he proceeded to spill a drop at a time down the long silken thread. As the deadly fluid was inches away from the lips of Nobunaga, the lord turned suddenly to his side and awoke just in time to see what was happening. Goemon had to make a run for his life and barely escaped. Before this intrepid ninja had another chance to attempt to fulfil his mission the evil Nobunaga was slain at the hands of someone else. Such was the importance of the ninja's mission that even his own death was of little consequence – as long as he was successful. The ninja's outlook towards death was about the only thing that they had in common with the Samurai. To both warrior castes death held no fear – it was just an occurrence. Over the centuries the myth of the ninja has grown, along with folklore and fiction. But one thing above all else is certain: the ninja warrior was a force to be reckoned with.

Petals of death

In another tale a certain ninja was sent out to kill the lord of Nagoya castle. But no matter how hard he tried the ninja just couldn't get near his target's private apartments. The lord's defences were such that he did not venture anywhere without a huge retinue of personal Samurai. Even when he slept, six Samurai were in the bed chamber, working on a rota of three awake and three asleep. Such security the ninja had never experienced before. The ninja knew he could not return unsuccessful, so some other method had to be devised. Week after week went by and the ninja kept a close watch on his target, looking for even the slightest break or alteration in the lord's routine that would give him the opportunity to make his move. From a vantage point deep in the foliage of a large tree the ninja watched the lord perform all his daily duties. He noticed that each morning and evening the lord took a stroll around his well-kept garden and seemed to pay particular attention to a huge rose bush. Without fail, every day the lord would stoop to smell each rose on the bush before returning to his duties. So the ninja hit upon a plan. In the late afternoon he sneaked into the garden and coated each rose with a deadly but sweet-smelling poison that once inhaled would bring instant death. At dusk, the lord made the usual rounds of his adored garden. As he stooped to smell the delicate perfume of the rose, he inhaled the deadly fumes and seconds later fell to the ground clutching at his throat. In a moment he was dead. The ninja had accomplished what he had been sent out to do, and escaped silently into the night.

Ninja Unarmed Combat Skills

Those who talk least hear the most

ALTHOUGH the ninja warrior was a walking arsenal, there were times when he could be caught without any weapon at all. It was on these occasions that to defend himself he had to rely on unarmed combat skills called *taijutsu*, which literally translated means 'body art'. Taijutsu forms the basis for all understanding in the fighting arts of ninjutsu.

Bonds of brotherhood

In today's martial arts it is taijutsu that is taught to prospective ninja students. Unlike the martial arts skills of karate and taekwondo, which are for the most part very competition orientated, ninjutsu offers a complete self-protection programme. The atmosphere in a ninja training hall promotes bonds of brotherhood, rather than students being in direct competition with one another and it is interesting that this approach is common all around the world in ninja training today. Many beginners, who come into ninjutsu training from other martial arts, often remark that they can feel and sense this friendly effusive air that pervades. The centre of all ninja training is located in Japan under the direct guidance of the art's grandmaster Dr Masaaki Hatsumi, who is the 34th grandmaster of the Togakure Ryu Ninja.

The four fighting positions

Unlike any other empty-hand Japanese system, taijutsu stresses body dynamics, the principle of using the whole of the body as a weapon. There is no basic fighting stance, which is always determined by the relationship of the fighter to his opponent. However, although this may appear to be something of a contradiction, there are actually four main fighting positions, but these are only used as a framework for the student so that he can gain an understanding of how taijutsu operates.

These four fighting positions are the natural stance, defensive stance, offensive stance and receiving stance. This last stance seems, at first glance, to have similarities with the aikido principle, which makes use of evasion and then countering. It is sometimes interpreted as inviting an attack, or misinterpreted as surrendering to one. This is because the practitioner stands in a relaxed manner with his arms and legs spread wide open, as though he were about to give in. As the attack commences, the taijutsu exponent appears to vanish, but then suddenly rises up behind the attacker, to mete out his own justice. Because taijutsu is strictly a combat martial art, the aim of its proponents is to inflict the greatest possible damage with the fewest moves and easiest methods. The art encompasses grappling, throws and escapes, locks, chokes, and muscle and bone attacks. All the time the student has to control the fight – once control is lost, so too is the fight itself.

The key to this efficient and effective movement is co-ordinated rhythm. For obvious reasons any encounter is a spontaneous and sudden action, requiring a response without even thinking. To enable the ninja student to train for this, special exercises were devised to act as a foundation. These are sparring, target-hitting, shadow boxing, and visualization. The first three are self-explanatory. The fourth, visualization, is employed to increase the student's awareness so he can assimilate the principles of various body movements. The aim is to visualize in the training hall the effects of certain attacks and counters under controlled conditions, thereby training the consciousness to develop a kind of sixth sense. The concept is that the student reads a situation before it happens, then he can never be surprised by an attack.

Anticipating the unexpected

Beginners start by learning to block and counter, but by the time the student gets to a higher grade his actions depend on where he happens to be at that particular time in body-positioning terms during a fight. When a student throws an adversary he never really knows where or how he is going to land. In taijutsu terms, the student can't determine the next move by stating he has to execute this particular arm-lock, or that particular hold. So in training students are given lots of exercises that involve moving from side to side in rapid succession. This develops a feeling of how an opponent will move or react when grabbed. This knowledge is then logged and students train repeatedly so that both movement and reaction become instinctual.

As training progresses some light sparring is introduced, but again it is pretty much a case of 'anything goes'. Kicks and strikes are delivered at a distance, then when the distance gap is closed, armlocks and short-range strikes are implemented. The instructor instils into the students that when they are sparring, it's not a 'win at all costs' situation but that they have to learn to take one or two knocks themselves, just to experience the feeling of being hit. Then in a life-or-death situation, the feeling of being hit won't come as too much of a shock and therefore distract them thus allowing it to become a weakness. In early training elaborate balancing manoeuvres are taught, which involve a light form of gymnastics. Students learn how to perform handstands while someone holds their legs. Movement, or more correctly body movement, is the key to ninjutsu's many techniques.

A continuous flowing motion

Apart from the four fighting positions previously mentioned, part of the platform from which students begin is introduced as the *ju mon gi no kamae*, (front stance) and *ichi mongi no kamae*, (back stance). Using these two very basic stances the student is taken through a set series of 18 techniques called *kamae no kata*. This sequence of movement teaches the student to flow from one position to another, and yet again into another and so on, but in a continuous smooth motion. The kamae no kata encompasses the basic techniques that a student first experiences in taijutsu unarmed combat training and it aids the beginner in linking up movements before he becomes adept at actually falling into an instinctive reactionary role from which to operate. It teaches the student to flow from left to right and assume fighting platforms or stances from which to execute attacks and counters. Using this set training programme allows the ninja student to further his training when he or she is not under the direct supervision of the instructor.

The basic techniques (*Kihon happo*) in taijutsu consist of three punching techniques, three one-handed grabs, and two two-handed grabs. Students perform these movements in pairs and they don't practise as though one side was trying to catch the other. They perform the techniques close up and are encouraged to help one another – thus maintaining the brotherhood of the art. The idea is to get the techniques to flow. Once the flow is perfected by the students, then they start to vary the techniques.

Throughout training it is emphasized that the student has to understand body manoeuvrability. Constant training brings an awareness to each student that a given course of action from an opponent can be easily evaded merely by moving their own body out of the way. So subtle is this art of taijutsu, that not even a block is needed to counter an attack from an adversary. Just by moving one way or another, repeated attacks can be stopped without the ninja student ever having to retaliate if they do not wish to.

Ninja Unarmed Combat Skills

Sensitivity awareness

Taijutsu training involves rolling techniques with breakfalls similar to those employed in judo. Cartwheels are another of the ninja's evasion body techniques, which when put into practice during an affray look quite amusing. One popular exercise that helps put a beginner in touch with his or her own body is blindfolded pushing. This involves a student being blindfolded and then having another student push them over. The person blindfolded has no idea from which direction the push is to be initiated, so it comes as a surprise. They then have to breakfall, roll over and come back up assuming a fighting position. As soon as the blindfolded person feels the 'contact' of the other person's body (their hands) pushing them, in an instant they go with it, riding the push and rolling to spring out of it lightly back on their feet. Repetitive training in this area gets the person used to feeling any kind of aggressive pressure from another quarter upon his own person. This type of training teaches balance and sensitivity awareness. Knowing what is going on around him, whether he can see or not, is all part and parcel of the ninja's perception.

Secret Art of the Ninja

The first level of learning

In the body art of taijutsu students have to be brought up to certain fitness levels before they become capable of initiating techniques. Therefore much of the early part of the instructional programme is spent in getting the beginner's body exercised and trained. The thinking behind this is that students vary from young to old, and everyone has a different physically active state of fitness. So movement and more movement is involved, aided by circuit training and exercises.

The student's first impressions are that taijutsu is a little like a jigsaw. But over the months and years of training it all begins to slot together, so that when a student arrives at the stage when he takes his proficiency examination, termed *shodan* (black belt), an overall picture of the art of taijutsu has begun to emerge. But even after a student reaches the black belt stage of competency, he has reached only the first level of learning. It can be equated with a driving test: passing your test doesn't make you an expert driver.

Many of the popular martial arts training systems attempt to mould the student's ways of reacting and moving to fit a stylized set of predetermined movements. Taijutsu works in the opposite manner by getting rid of the awkward or unnatural tendencies that may have been picked up unwittingly over the years and concentrating on natural movement. As a fighting system, taijutsu relies on natural body strength and resiliency, speed of response and movement and an understanding of the principles of nature for successful results in self-protection. Taijutsu techniques take advantage of natural physical construction and efficient employment of body dynamics. Although most of these underlying theories are predominantly Chinese in origin (which recent research and discoveries have proven), many distinct subtle changes have been made along the way. For instance, unlike in many kung-fu styles, students of taijutsu need not imitate kinds of animals or distort or deform their body structure to employ the techniques. It is interesting to note that the principles behind the body mechanics of taijutsu also provide the foundation for combat with the weapon arts of ninjutsu.

Strength through flexibility

Another integral component of taijutsu is called *junan taiso* (body conditioning). The exercises within this framework contribute to the suppleness, speed and responsive action necessary for the effective application of taijutsu techniques. In training, strength is generated through flexibility. The muscles and joints are exercised to enhance their natural elastic qualities, and not to stretch, strain or tear, as is seen in many other martial arts disciplines. Junan taiso's basic exercise plan institutes a correct and balanced diet which ultimately provides for strength, flexibility and health in general – another indication that the original system has all the hallmarks of being Chinese.

During the practice of the junan taiso exercises, it can be observed that the body tissue, fluid circulation, breathing patterns, and active direction of the consciousness are all in harmony with each other. By learning the effects and influences of the body's many maintenance systems, the student of ninjutsu can develop a working knowledge of his or her own power, to control the health and condition of the body. When attacked, the ninja fights from his basic position – called *ichimonji*. This pose is assumed as the body slides back away from the attack. The back leg carries most of the weight and the leading leg holds the body upright. The shoulders are held low and relaxed with the hands in the open-palm position protecting the face and body. Specific ninja taijutsu techniques number in their thousands and include countless variations on a given theme. Ninja students are not expected to learn all of these techniques, but rather work on internalizing the principles embodied by them.

Ninja Unarmed Combat Skills

Handling any situation

Spontaneity, or automatically reacting with the appropriate action to the elements of the circumstances, is a crucial skill for self-defence. The ninja student is prepared to adapt to any situation that confronts him and is not tempted to force the situation to fit the parameters of some specialized training system – which again highlights the differences between ninjutsu and other popular martial arts. The broad scope of ninja training has therefore evolved to include methods to handle any situation. The martial arts student who is only trained to punch will encounter great difficulty in situations where his punching skills are ineffective or inappropriate. True proficiency in self-defence comes from a blending of all areas of skill with the body, and cannot result from the dangerous and limiting concept of developing a speciality, which if it fails leaves the person wide open to counter-movements from an aggressor.

The body knows how to move if we let it and does not require active mental control to respond properly in a threatening situation. The student of taijutsu works to eliminate the awkward process of first mechanically thinking through a response before actually carrying it out.

Ninjutsu's natural stance involves quite simply standing in a relaxed manner with the arms loosely hanging by the sides. The knees are straight but not locked back. This position employs the ninja earth principle. The second stance is the defensive posture, which is used to counter the opponent's techniques. The emphasis on this posture is to let the hips move first, with the body following. This posture employs the ninja water principle of being fluid. The third position is the offensive posture, best described as slightly similar to that of a boxer's stance. The ninja in this position moves forward to meet his attacker, the power coming from the trunk of the body and not the shoulders. The fire element is this position's principle. The last posture is the receiving stance. In this amazing position the ninja quite literally stands spread-eagled, arms and legs spread wide apart, looking foolishly open to any attack under the sun. But, like the art it belongs to, this position is very deceiving. Based on the ninja principle of the wind, this receiving pose makes use of evasion.

Awarding progress

All training in taijutsu is practised in a standard black suit. Examinations are taken at varying intervals to judge and assess the student's progress in the system and the knowledge he or she has accumulated during training. Coloured belts are awarded (as is usual in all Japanese martial arts) when a student is successful in passing the set test. All beginners start off with a white belt, which ultimately leads to the shodan. Along the way there are nine stages to be completed. The first grade is termed *kyu* and is identified by a green belt, which is superseded as proficiency increases by the next grade downwards, i.e. 8th, 7th, 6th, and so on.

In ninjutsu the green coloured belt only changes when the student becomes a black belt, unlike other Japanese martial arts where the colours change according to grade. To identify the degrees of proficiency of the lower grades a star is awarded which is then sewn on to the official badge of the organization. These stars are silver and each grade passed adds another to the badge until the student has four, which will then make him a 4th kyu. From this stage the star colour changes to gold, four of these stars being required for the student to take his black belt examination and consequently become an instructor himself although the learning of the art continues for a lifetime.

All kyu grades wear a badge with the Japanese calligraphy for ninjutsu emblazoned upon it in white on a red background with a white border. The *dan* (black belt badge) carries black calligraphy on a red background with a white border. Taijutsu's grading system, the same all over the world, was instituted at the Japanese headquarters of grandmaster Dr Masaaki Hatsumi.

Secret Art of the Ninja

Students of ninjutsu

Because ninjutsu is relatively new in the West, instructors are a little thin on the ground, but once a beginner finds a ninja group (it is always called a group not a club) the would-be student is interviewed by the instructor as to why they want to learn the art. If the instructor is satisfied with the reasons, the new student is formally introduced to the rest of the class, which is often termed 'the family'. All ninja training has one primary objective – to free the practitioner from a rigid training structure. It is believed that following a set course limits the student and eventually strangles him in technique for technique's sake. The aim is, through technique, to achieve total freedom of self-expression. This theory is quite the opposite of that underlying the conventional martial arts' training methods. As has been stated earlier, kung fu, karate and taekwondo all rest on a firm foundation of basic techniques that serve as the building blocks which every practitioner must use if they wish to become an adept.

Ninjutsu as we have seen is somewhat different. Although the so-called basics are there as a guide for beginner students, they are only used as starters or spring boards to allow the student to become comfortable within a martial arts discipline. Each new student grasps these bare fundamentals with this sole

Ninja Unarmed Combat Skills

aim in mind. For many people ninjutsu eventually becomes a way of life.

The new students of ninjutsu starts by learning how to use their body to the best advantage, not just parts of thebody, like the arms or legs, but all of it. They undergo junan taiso which teaches them how to become supple. The ninja rely purely upon natural body movement for effective self-defence. Their exercise regimen is designed to relax the muscles, not wear them out through prolonged conditioning.

A typical training exercise might begin with the students lying on their backs, with their hands clasped behind the head and the legs extended. Twisting the body from this position, they then bring the right elbow down to meet the rising left knee. This whole procedure is repeated about ten times. A single breath is released throughout the exercise, inhaling only taking place again when the body has returned to the ground. This exercise strengthens the lower torso and the waist. Many many other exercises are implemeted, all aimed at preparing the students' bodies for the work (techniques) to come later.

In empty-handed combat ninjutsu aims to become proficient in every possible situation, defensive or offensive. No distinctions are made according to whether the attacker be heavier or lighter, smaller or larger, or weaker or stronger. The system had to work in all cases for the ninja to survive. The taijutsu element is thus an all round method for using the body's natural movement to avoid being hit, while at the same time preparing the defender for counter attack. Students train in every branch of the art in order to arrive at a spontaneous fighting mode which allows them to defend themselves in any situation.

Body familiarity

Taijutsu rests on a concept of body familiarity that takes the practitioner beyond what they perhaps thought was possible. As we have seen, when attacked, a practitioner can place themselves out of harm's way simply by shifting their weight from one foot to another. And without adopting a static pose, they remain in a position to retaliate. Since the art of ninjutsu began, set stances have never been used. Subtle shifts in body weight and foot positioning seem to neutralize all kinds of attacks. The defender appears to envelop the attacker without exerting themselves in any way. As an old Chinese saying puts it, 'Deviate an inch, and lose a thousand miles'.

In other words averting a strike by an inch is as good as averting it by a mile. Ninjutsu practitioners scorn the excessive energy and movement which the other martial arts put into a block or evasion. In nin-jutsu every confrontation is unique; methods of counter-offensive strikes cannot be worked out beforehand. And the taijutsu use of the body is the unifying key between all of the techniques.

The Modern-Day Ninja

The highest branch is not always the safest roost

AS the 20th century winds towards its close, the world's global community is witnessing more and more chaos both in society and at the very roots of its government. International terrorism is rife, assassination, both political and civil, is commonplace. The world's military and law-enforcement agencies are having to recruit and train specialized personnel who are best equipped to deal with the worsening situation. These elite groups of fighters or security forces are delving into the past for their training methods in an effort to combat and neutralize the destructive elements that exist in our society.

Bloody showdown in London

Much of the advanced training is obviously very secret, but one wonders if the ancient art of ninjutsu is still very much alive and kicking in the special service units secret training camps, creating a type of modern ninja armed with the very latest technological weapons and forming the super-ninja units of tomorrow. The art of ninjutsu is a system encompassing almost limitless conflict techniques and weaponry principles which can be adapted to almost any clandestine conflict anywhere in the world – from the deserts of Saudi Arabia to Central American jungle camps. In the United States Defense Department analysts have studied ninjutsu techniques and history to such an extent that they have evolved a tactical treatise based upon the art of the ancient ninja.

One recent political incident whch called for the use of ninjutsu techniques was the assault on the Iranian Embassy, known infamously as the siege of Princes Gate, in London on 30 April 1980.

A group of terrorists, members of the Mohieddin al Nasser, an Arab martyr group who were intent upon seeking liberation for their country Khuzestan, stormed the Iranian embassy and held 26 hostages at gunpoint. Their demands were autonomy for Khuzestan and the immediate release of 91 of their fellow countrymen held in Iranian jails.

By the third day of the siege, police negotiators had made no progress and an SAS infiltration reconnaissance team was sent into the arena. They climbed upon the roof of the Ethiopian Embassy next door at number 18 and gained entrance to the premises. They quickly and silently began to break down the dividing wall by removing bricks one at a time. Then they waited while all the different governmental factions negotiated with the terrorists to see if a settlement could be achieved without the use of force.

However, when on Monday May 5th nervous gunmen rattled off three shots, killing the Iranian press attaché, the Prime Minister gave permission for the SAS to go in and break the siege.

Over a hundred television companies from all around the world focused their lenses on the embassy door as suddenly black-clad men appeared all over the place. The plan, code-named Operation Nimrod, was to take the building from three sides. The SAS abseiled from the roof and within seconds fixed explosive charges to the bullet-proof glass window frames on the balcony. Through the then shattered glass they threw in stun grenades. At their moment of entry the other SAS teams entered the building from their designated positions. For the next few minutes explosions and gunfire could be heard from all parts of the building. Palls of smoke gushed from the broken windows. Then suddenly it was all over. The SAS Counter-Revolutionary force had been successful. As everyone was congratulating each other for a job well done and the press converged onto the street, the SAS were nowhere to be seen. They had somehow just disappeared like shadows in the mist.

The siege, which had begun at 11.25am that morning, had been broken in only 18 minutes. All the terrorists but one had been shot and killed and the world applauded the daring exploits of Great Britain's SAS. Perfect planning, good reconnaissance, use of state-of the art technology, (listening devices, bugs) precision timing, total focus on the job at hand and superb training of the personnel were all mitigating factors in ensuring that Operation Nimrod became a text book perfect assault on the Iranian Embassy.

The whole scenario could have been taken from Sun Tsu's *Art of War*. In fact the personnel could almost have been ninja warriors from 15th-century Japan. The special units of the world's armed forces have certainly looked to history and gleaned valuable information for use today in the war against international terrorism.

The Modern-Day Ninja

The skills of the shadow warriors

Certain elements in the Iranian Embassy siege relate to the ninja's exploits in medieval Japan. The SAS are service personnel who are schooled in the basic training of the armed services. They then can choose to go for 'Selection' into one of the specialist or covert branches of the military. Intensive training in aspects of covert warfare is carried out and techniques in espionage, survival and the use of weapons are studied. This training takes up to six months or more before a select few are deemed competent enough to take their place within the specialized units. Almost 95 per cent fail selection and sadly return to their ranks within the ordinary services. The special 5 per cent will then undergo further training and then perhaps select the area of expertise they wish to concentrate upon. The whole training programme takes about two years. As we have seen, the finished product is a fighting elite the likes of which cleared and broke the siege in London in 18 minutes.

Can you possibly imagine the competence and skills of a person who has undergone such training on a daily basis for almost 20 years? Such a person was the ninja, who trained with the very best weapons masters, covert and espionage teachers, survival experts, and a whole range of other skilled experts for ten times as long as the SAS train in today's modern army. Is it little wonder that the ninja gained such a frightening reputation among the peasants and Samurai alike? Add to this that in those times barely 10 per cent of the whole population of the country could read or write, religious dogma was rife, movement and travel within the country was strictly controlled, superstition ruled the peasant's life. The appearance or even rumour of a ninja operating in a district must have presented a veritable spectre of doom to all concerned.

To a 20th-century audience many of the exploits of the ninja may seem a little dubious, far fetched and more fiction than fact. But in reality they were probably more adept, more sinister, more amazing than we could ever know. Their art is an art of espionage and secrecy, so it would stand to reason that much of what they did has been lost in the annals of time. When the clans died or simply faded away their secrets went with them, lost for ever. There is not much written that would do credit to the skills of these Shadow Warriors of yesteryear. But if the clans did survive past the Second World War then they have followed the ancient dictates of the ninja by going underground and once again shrouding themselves in secrecy.

The art of winning

Ninjutsu has become more than just a martial art: its development through the ages has reached the point where the art actually embraces life itself. The city executive or businessman about to embark on a deal – all can gain something from the qualities that ninjutsu has to offer. As the Western authority on the system Shidoshi Stephen Hayes once said, 'Ninjutsu is the art of winning'. Built within the modern framework of teaching, the art no longer instructs its adepts to skulk around in the dead of night, but allows the student, no matter what the circumstances, to interpret the techniques freely and use them accordingly whether they apply to taijutsu in a street self-defence situation, or to the psychological aspects of the art in a boardroom battle.

Movie superheroes

Recent trends in ninjutsu ensure that the art of the ninja is going to be with us for a long time into the future. Hollywood, through the celluloid image, has perpetuated the lifestyle of these shadow warriors and depicted them as superheroes transposed from Japan's dark feudal past into the 20th century. In the 1980s the television industry produced a series called *The Master*, starring Lee van Cleef. Almost overnight the name ninja became a household word, just as kung-fu became one back in the early 1970s when the late Bruce Lee burst onto the scene. It is interesting to note that apart from the many students who train in the martial art of ninjutsu around the world, there exists a quite separate group of individuals who can be termed 'ninja enthusiasts'. These devotees, however, are not interested in learning the ancient skills of the art, but merely follow the ways of the ninja by donning black uniforms and face masks and acting out some of the escapades of the shinobi warriors in the privacy of their own homes.

Some martial artists have taken to the acting profession and people such as Chuck Norris and Sho Kosugi made such movies as *Nine Deaths of the Ninja*, *Ninja 3 the Domination* and *The Octagon*. A few years ago a relatively unknown star named David Dudikoff had a huge box office hit with the film *American Ninja*.

The grandmaster's successor

But what has happened to the ninja in Japan? Most of the ninjutsu taught in the world today emanates from a quiet suburb of Noda City in Chiba prefecture. It is here that the present grandmaster of the art, Dr Masaaki Hatsumi, has his *dojo* (school). Hatsumi *sensei* (teacher) is a bone-setter by profession but a ninjutsu teacher par excellence by succession. The

The Modern-Day Ninja

title of grandmaster was bestowed upon him by the late 33rd grandmaster and Hatsumi's own instructor, sensei Toshitsugu Takamatsu. Until that time (1972) no Westerner had ever been taught the art. In fact, in his earlier days Hatsumi sensei used to train in ninjutsu dressed in a white suit similar to those used in karate and judo, just to disguise what he was practising. Toshitsugu Takamatsu was totally against anyone other than a Japanese learning the art. So, in effect, Dr Hatsumi broke with tradition slightly when he opened up instruction to Europeans and Americans.

Ninja tradition dictates that even now Dr Hatsumi will be looking for a successor to become the 35th grandmaster. It is a long process of knowing and learning, and finding a person with the suitable qualities required to assume leadership. If, by chance, he cannot find an heir, he will destroy all his scrolls and his own personal ninja weapons. He will leave nothing behind him. This is the strict clan code and system, which dates back nearly 800 years to the first founder of the ninja Togakure system, *soke* Daisuke Togakure, the Japanese word *soke* meaning founder of a school or system. If and when Dr Hatsumi finds a successor from among his many world-wide schools, that person will be unaware of his future role. Unbeknown to him he will be groomed in the ninja ways and traditions and singled out for special skills training. He will learn all that is required of him to become, one day, the 35th grandmaster of ninjutsu.

Survive or die

The modern world has spawned another application for the ninja arts. With the threat of global nuclear war hanging over us like a Damaclesian sword, a world-wide movement is beginning to grow, its adherents known as Survivalists. Its devotees train with great intent to ensure they will survive a nuclear holocaust. Although paramilitary in appearance, these private clubs and organizations have examined in great detail the lifestyle of the ancient ninja warriors, whom they consider to be the ultimate survivalists. Consequently, ninja training methods are being studied and extended to fit their activities. Because of the obvious problems that a nuclear disaster would bring, such as the breakdown of law and order, roving bands of robbers would comb the countryside pillaging in an effort to stay alive. The survivalists maintain that for themselves and their families to manage under such circumstances, personal defence will take priority.

The three levels of thought

Ninja theories can also teach survival in everyday life. The ninja concept is to approach survival in life at three levels, the first level being actual outdoor survival in such circumstances as a car breakdown miles from anywhere, or a person being lost in the wilds far from civilization. Most countries in the winter months in the western hemisphere experience drastic weather conditions and it is not unknown for drivers to be found frozen to death in their cars. A little knowledge of how to stay calm, keep warm and dry, and recognize what herbs and plants give sustenance, can make all the difference between living and dying. The art of ninjutsu teaches how to cope in such situations: ultimately to make you a survivor rather than a statistic. Being a survivor means coping with a given situation when all hope has gone, so the ninja arts extend beyond their martial possibilities.

At the second level of thought, ninja training teaches to adept a way of survival thinking. If you can plan ahead, then you don't have to worry about danger. In simple terms, the long length of nylon cord in the boot of your car, perhaps an extra blanket, maybe even some tinned or dried food packs – even an emergency first-aid kit – could make all the difference. You are ready for the unexpected and will be able to cope. All this creates a more organized life: being prepared without getting too paranoid about it.

The third level of ninja survival training hits out at the very heart of daily life. The conscious sense of awareness spills over from the first two levels and creates a pattern to help you run your own life. The student begins to conduct a well-ordered and pre-pared life, the first two levels becoming symbols of the third. The student learns that he does not have to waste his energy with negative thoughts and attitudes when they arise. This is not to say that the problems we may face in life should be just brushed under the carpet or forgotten about. In life, we may all have a major problem to face. But by preparing for the eventuality, we can lose the negative aspects by focus-ing and channelling all our energies directly at the major problem rather than wasting them by handling those things which should have been foreseen.

Opening the Mind

This awareness could almost be called 'the power of positive thinking'. In modern day ninja training, especially at higher levels, the student is encouraged to follow spiritual paths to facilitate greater under-standing of life.

This may seem something of a paradox if we con-sider the early development of the ninja and their art of the silent assassin. But for such an art as ninjutsu to have survived down the eons of time a certain amount of growth and evolution had to occur. Let us not forget the book that purportedly started it all, Sun Tsu's *Art of War*. At face value it, too, is a manual for waging war with a code of directives that allow all manner of mayhem and murder to achieve their aim. But if you look deeper into the underlying philosophy of this ancient text you realize that the greatest achievement of all is to win without fighting. As Sun Tsu states, 'The supreme act of war is to subdue the enemy without fighting.'

Ninjutsu follows the Chinese dualities of the Yin and Yang, in Japanese and ninjutsu it is termed In and Yo. Westerners may be more familiar with the circular symbol of the two fishes, one all black with a tiny white eye, and one all white with a tiny black eye. This symbol is meant to represent the balance within nature, the universe and man. Anything that is perceived as all bad cannot be totally bad, hence the black fish with the white eye. And vice versa. There is always a balance .

It is said that to understand this process of interaction is to understand life itself. For whatever reasons the ninja arose to prominence they would not have remained there for so long had the need for them not been there. Just like the battlefield skills of the martial arts which were devised for killing an enemy when all weapons were lost, so ninjutsu has evolved from an assassins' art to a modern-day method of discovering yourself and your true potential through specialized training.

This is at the crux of modern day ninjutsu training. It is no longer about learning how to kill silently or how to become trained in terrorist principles of sabotage. It is about perfecting your own gifts as a human being within the ever-changing universe. It is about developing not just the physical but also the mental and psychological. The disciplines taught within the fighting and weapon aspects of the art are merely paths meant to direct the individual student to higher learning. This is not learning as traditionally

The eight trigrams which form the basis for the Chinese book of divination called the *I-Ching*. These eight trigrams all have an attribute which can be further broken down into 64 hexagrams. Seen in the centre is the symbol known as the **yin-yang** which always indicates the continuous flowing force of the universe, which the ninja tapped into during their meditative moment when channelling energy.

envisaged through academic study but learning by contacting the inner child and elevating spiritual needs and aspirations. The Indian Yoga systems teach, through a series of various contorted movements of the body, certain principles that are said to prolong longevity, and prevent illness. These principles are platforms to the Eastern way of elevating consciousness and opening the mind to further thought. A whole system of breathing exercises and diet accompanies these Yogi systems .

The power within

Modern ninjutsu encompasses all these practical and psychological aspects and programmes them into its training curriculum. It could even be said that there is a fourth level of survival, which teaches the student that he has the power within himself to overcome fears. He learns that by building up personal objectives without setting higher limits, he can create within his mind a feeling of success, an air of positivity about his life. Once he has successfully made this step, the momentum it creates gradually begins to develop into a positive attitude and a mental awareness of situations. Just knowing his capabilities – that he can overcome limits and create successes out of what, to other people, are terrifying conditions – ultimately leads the ninja adept to overcome the unknown fear of his mind.

Then all is possible. It is this level of training that takes ninjutsu to its higher order of ideals and enlightenment.

The test of truth

Much of the development of modern ninjutsu in the West has been due mainly to the efforts of three men: Andrew Adams, an American martial arts journalist, whose book *The Invisible Assassins* whetted the appetites of the masses for the ninja and their secret art; Stephen Hayes, the first American ninja who introduced the art to the USA and then to the rest of the world; and the unsung hero of this group, who in true ninja style seemed to want to remain in the shadows, an Israeli called Doron Novon.

It was Novon who first went to Japan to train under Dr Hatsumi personally, and who became the highest-graded Westerner in the arts of ninjutsu. When after many years training he took his fifth dan he had to undergo more than just a simple test of training competency. Being a fifth dan meant that he had reached a higher order of the *ninpo* (spiritual training) ladder and had to pass what was termed 'The Test of Truth'. The first non-Japanese to take this ultimate test of the Togakure ninjutsu system, he sat cross-legged with his back to grandmaster Hatsumi. The master raised his sword above his head, and then, suddenly, struck at the head of Doron Novon.

The Modern-Day Ninja

In times gone by, a real sword was used. Today, however, a *bokken* or wooden sword is used, but the blow, if felt, while not fatal, is still an extremely painful experience. Only a split second separates the student and the deadly blow. If the student can feel or sense the sword coming down and escape, he passes the test. If he fails ...

Until that day, only five of Hatsumi sensei's students had passed the test on their first attempt. In a hushed silence in front of all the other ninja masters Doron Novon took the test. Without any prior warning Hatsumi struck, with not even a change of breath to indicate his movement. The heavy hardwood sword moved at lightning speed towards the skull of the seated Israeli. Within the wink of an eye, it was as if someone, or some unseen force or saviour, had pulled Novon aside. The wooden sword merely sliced through the air and down to the floor, making no contact with anything but the bamboo matting. Novon had passed The Test of Truth and made history at the same time. Such is the power of the mind at the higher levels of training in the art of ninjutsu.

The legend lives on

For all its traditions of secrecy over the centuries, ninjutsu is still very much alive and in the hands of martial artists who constantly train to attain higher ideals and standards of experiencing life to the full. But one may often wonder in this competitive world of ours, when industrial secrets go missing, or a seized political hostage is suddenly and mysteriously released, if one of the modern-day shadow warriors of the night has been responsible...

Glossary

Amur River

East Asian river formed by the Argun and Shilka rivers. The Amur river enters the Sea of Okhotsk. An ultra-nationalist society named its secret organization the Amur River Society when in 1901 they were convinced that Japan would have to fight Russia. Also known as the Kokuryukai or the Black Dragon Society. Its main purpose is espionage and sabotage.

Art of War

Book on strategy by Sun Tsu purported to have been written over 3,000 years ago. First translated from Chinese into French by a Jesuit priest named Father Amiot in 1782. First English translation by P.F.

Glossary

Calthrop in 1905. Legend relates that this book was also a bible to the ninja clans.

Aruki

The ninja skill of 'Stealth Walking'. Allowed ninja warrior to move silently and undetected around castle corridors. Due to their great age the wooden floors in Japanese medieval fortresses squeaked quite loudly when pressure was put upon them. The skill in Aruki lies in the practitioner's ability to use their body weight in unison with their floor manoeuvrability.

Also known as **Yoko Aruki** meaning sideways walking.

Ashikaga

Takauji Ashikaga became the first real Shogun of Japan, he set up his government in Kamakura in 1339. It was known as the Ashikaga Shogunate.

Bakufu

Literal meaning 'Camp Office'. A military system of national administration. First set up in the 12th century. The Bakufu and its ruling power the Shogun relegated the emperor to almost puppet status.

Glossary

Bisento

Spear-like weapon with a blade resembling a scimitar fixed to its end; much favoured by the ninja.

Black Ships

Term given by the Japanese to the sailing ships of Commodore Matthew Perry, the American naval officer who commanded an expedition to Japan in 1853 and reopened communication between Japan and the outside world after Japan's self imposed 250-year isolation policy. Through Commodore Perry the treaty of Kanagawa (1854) was arbitrated to give the USA trading rights with Japan.

Bo

6 foot (1.8m) wooden staff, around which is built a complete fighting system, and which can be likened to the old English quarterstaff.

Bodhidharma

The Indian holy man, also known as Ta'mo and Daruma, who is credited with bringing Zen Buddhism to China where it was known as Ch'an Buddhism. It became known as Zen when the religion reached Japan. This austere method of Buddhism was much favoured by the Samurai warrior. The Zen

Glossary

concepts of the Samurai are still very much favoured in Japan today.

Buddhism

Religious doctrine founded in India by the philosopher Siddhartha Gautama (Buddha). In ancient times it was closely connected to the practice of kung-fu, through the Buddhist monks who helped develop the art in China.

Budo

Literally meaning Warrior way or Way of the warrior.

Bujinkan

Ninja training hall or club *dojo*. Also the name for Masaaki Hatsumi's organization.

Bushi

Means Martial Man, a Japanese term indicating a warrior who follows the code of Bushido – the ethical code of the Samurai which stressed honour, loyalty, duty and obedience. Understanding this Bushido concept can give great insight into the thinking of the Japanese businessmen of today.

Glossary

Caltrops

Sharp metal spiked weapon for throwing in the pathway of pursuers. Often the tips were poisoned. Natural caltrops used were the spiked shells of the water chestnut fruit. Also known as *tetsubishi*.

Chiba prefecture

Home of Dr Masaaki Hatsumi, the present grandmaster of the Tokagure ninjutsu system.

Chunin

Literally means 'middle person'. The second of the three military ranks in the ninja hierarchy. The *chunin* set the mission for the field ninja to carry out, and was ultimately responsible for its success.

Commando

The term originated in 19th-century South Africa with the Boers. An Afrikaans word. Boer Kommandos went behind enemy lines in small highly trained groups to raid the British during the Boer war.

Also British army raiding unit raised in the Second World War by Admiral Sir Roger Keyes. They, like many other elite paramilitary units, have been likened to the ninja of Japan because of their intensive training methods and modus operandi. The army commandos were disbanded at the end of the Second World War but their role was taken over and carried on by the Royal Marines.

Daikon

Giant Japanese white radish which grows abundantly and has great nutritional value, much used by the ninja while out on missions and living off the land.

Daimyo

Japanese feudal lords.

Daito

Japanese long sword with a cutting edge measuring over 25 inches used by the Samurai.

Daisho

The matching set of Japanese long and short swords, worn by all Samurai in the Tokugawa era.

Dan

Japanese for degree, denoting rank of black belt.

Dojo

The 'place of the way' – a training hall or gymnasium where martial arts are practised.

Glossary

Doshin-So

The founder of the Shorinji kempo martial art. It was greatly influenced by Chinese systems and is registered in Japan as a religious sect. It has been suggested that Doshin-So had connections with the Amur River Society.

Eastern Capital

The literal translation of Tokyo, the present-day capital of Japan.

En-no-Gyoja

Yamabushi or mountain warrior ascetic who tried to restore order in Japan in the 6th century by propagating a new way of Buddhism which was called Shugendo.

Fu

Ninja method of acting like the 'wind'. Fu is a method of fighting in the ninja body art of taijutsu and is characterized by harmonious interaction with other elements. It gives the user of the fu approach the appearance of being everywhere at the same time.

Glossary

Fudo ken

Ninja clenched fist used for punching and striking body targets.

Fugu *see* **Globefish**

Fujiwara

The Japanese military dynasty who were the real rulers of Japan throughout most of the Heian period. They ruled as regents from AD967 to AD1068 and gained access to the imperial throne through inter-marriage.

Fukiya

Pins and poisoned darts shot through a blow-gun at an unsuspecting enemy. Greatly used by many of the ninja clans during stealth activities.

Genin

Japanese for 'low person'. A genin was a ninja of the lowest rank and the one responsible for actually carrying out the mission. Also called a ninja, although ninja was the collective term for all three levels in the ninja hierarchy.

Glossary

Globefish

Known also as the blowfish or *fugu*. Its deadly poison (tetradoxin)was used by the ninja to tip darts and spikes for a faster and more effective kill. Considered today in Japan as something of a delicacy. Chefs that prepare the fugu fish dish have to undergo special training and become licensed by the government.

Go-Daigo

An emperor of Japan during the much troubled Kamakura period, overthrown by the Minamoto clan chief Takauji Ashikaga who had once been his ally.

Goton-po

Ninja's five principles of evasion, involving camouflage techniques and concealment tricks by blending in with the natural surroundings of the environment.

Green belt

Standard colour of belt used mostly in the grading examination of ninjutsu to differentiate the novices from the teachers.

Glossary

Gyoja

Warrior ascetics who lived in the remote mountainous regions of Japan. These wilderness people lived in caves and practised many of the esoteric and supernatural arts that were later taught to the ninja.

Hanbo

Ninja 3 foot (1m) staff or stick, *han* meaning half, and *bo* meaning staff. This weapon is used prolifically in modern ninjutsu training.

Hara-Kiri

Literal translation 'belly cut' proper name 'Seppuku'. Japanese traditional ritual suicide by disembowlment. It was the ultimate act of atonement for the ancient Samurai warrior who had lost his honour or respect.

Hatsumi

Dr Masaaki Hatsumi, the present leader and 34th grandmaster of the Tokagure ninja.

Hanzo Hattori

Clan chief of the Iga ninja in feudal Japan, was responsible for the founding of the early Japanese secret service.

Glossary

Heiho

Study of military strategy; one of the training skills a ninja had to master.

Hojo Family

Japanese dynasty. The family ruled as *Shikken* (regents) for the Shogun. The Bakufu was passed on to the Hojo family via the widow of Yorimoto Minamoto.

Hojo-Jutsu

The Japanese art of binding or rope tying. Adepts learn intricate methods of tying up a person with cord. First used by the ninja and Samurai alike. Some of the many hundreds of different types of knots and knot-tying learned could virtually ensnare a prisoner to the extent that even with a knife the almost Gordian like entanglement would have been difficult to escape from.

Hombu

Headquarters. This term can be used to define any headquarters for a martial arts school. It is the head or main training place of a martial arts system.

Glossary

Hypnotism

Long before Friedrich Mesmer discovered the method of artificially inducing a person to a state of relaxation in which suggestions or ideas can then be proposed to the hypnotee, the ninja via their mystic teachings were practising such methods. In South East Asia trance like states, whether artificially induced or through self hypnosis have been commonplace for millennia.

Iai Jutsu

This is a typically Samurai battlefield art which involves the practitioner rapidly drawing his sword to kill an opponent, and then just as quickly replacing the sword back into its scabbard. This art is still very much practised today although there is an emphasis on Zen in its practice. The art today is known as Iaido.

Iga

Remote area in feudal Japan where the ninja lived and trained. It is situated on the main island of Honshu.

Glossary

Goemon Ishikawa

Romantic ninja figure who is much glamorized in Japanese children's tales and is looked upon in a similar vein to a Robin Hood type character. Ishikawa was something of a lone ninja figure rather than one operating from a clan or family.

Jesuits

The Jesuits were the first to introduce Christianity to Japan under their leader St Francis Xavier in 1549. He arrived at Kagoshima in Kyushu to set up a mission. During their time in Japan the Jesuits were much involved in court intrigues and internal politics. They also worked upon securing trading agreements from the Shogun for the benefit of Spain.

Jonin

Ninja leader who negotiated with the feudal lords over ninja missions and fees exacted.

Jujitsu

A Japanese martial art in which the opponent's strength is turned against him. The art contains both armed and unarmed techniques. The term means soft or flexible. All Samurai were adept in at least one of the many forms or styles of jujitsu that were about at the time.

Jutte or Jitte

A single tined iron truncheon used by the early Japanese police force. The single tine at the hilt of the weapon enables the user to trap a *katana* (sword) without being injured by the blade. The ninja of later centuries found much use for this weapon.

Ka

Ninja fire posture.

Kaginawa

Ninja weapon consisting of a rope with a huge hook on the end for scaling walls and also for entangling a sword-wielding enemy.

Kama

The Kama was an agricultural implement , similar to a sickle, for cutting crops and grass. The blade was honed to razor sharpness by the ninja and used with deadly efficiency. Usually used in pairs.

Kamae

General term for a fighting posture.

Glossary

Kantokusha

Male commander of *kunoichi* (female ninja).

Katana

The correct term to use for a japanese sword.

Kendo

Modern Japanese fencing based upon the ancient Samurai skill and art of Kenjutsu. Today for safety reasons within the sporting form the live blade is substituted for a bamboo equivalent called *Shinai*. *Kendo* means way of the sword.

Ki

This is the Japanese translation of the Chinese word 'Chi', the vital energy within the human body. Development of Ki is an important part of the martial arts such as Aikido. The Ki power of the ninja, which was developed from a very early age took on almost frightening proportions when used as a psychological weapon. It is said that the ninja would test their Ki power by shouting at birds in the trees using the Kiai shout and the birds would fall stunned to the ground. The Kiai shout today can been heard in training halls of martial arts the world over.

Glossary

Koga

Province in Japan that supported many ninja clans. Along with the Iga ninja clans, the Koga ninja were among the most powerful of all the ninja clans.

Koppojutsu

Bone-breaking techniques of ninjutsu.

Kuji-kiri

Mystical finger-knitting patterns of the ninja. Kuji means the number nine. The ninja used this method to channel energy to conjure up their intrinsic powers. Also known as kuji-in.

Kunoichi

Female ninja agent.

Kusarifundo

Short weighted chain – a ninja ensnarement weapon.

Kusarigama

Chain and sickle weapon of the ninja.

Glossary

Kyoketsu shoge

Early ninja weapon consisting of a length of cord with a metal ring attached to one end and a pointed implement such as a knife attached to the other.

Kyudo

The way of the bow; the Japanese martial art of archery steeped in the principles of Zen. Great emphasis is attached to the practitioner's attitude and to the way he or she fires the arrow. Actually hitting the target they are aiming at is of little consequence. Considered a great past-time with the Samurai and still practised today in modern Japan.

Makiwara

A striking post used for conditioning the hands and feet. Repeated use builds up rock hard callouses on the knuckles and the ball of the feet. If caught without weapons the ninja would resort to his unarmed combat methods and death blows are easily obtained from a strike from their calloused hands aimed to a vital organ.

Metsubushi

Ninja blinding powder, often thrown at opponents to distract and blind them; it was also blown through a hollow bamboo tube when fighting at close quarters for a more accurate effect. Ground spices or finely ground pottery were just some of the types of powders used in such a manner.

Mikado

The Western term used to denote the Emperor of Japan. The word means 'Exalted Gate'.

Mikkyo

Secret doctrines of Shugendo Buddhism. These teachings are said to have originated in Tibet.

Minamoto

Arguably the Minamoto family was the most powerful clan in Japan. The great Shogun Ieyasu was a direct descendent. It was he who was responsible for shutting down Japan to the outside world for nearly 250 years. Although he abdicated two years after he took the shogunate and his son Hidetada took his place, this did little to take the real power from his machinations. As a direct result of Ieyasu's governing the ninja clans began their great decline.

Glossary

Momochi Sandayu

Momochi, ninja clan leader and teacher of Goemon Ishikawa, the famous bandit hero of Japan.

Muromachi

This is the name of the period of the Ashikaga Shogunate which lasted from 1339 to 1573, named after a district in the then capital of Japan Kyoto.

Naginata

Spear-like weapon with a curved blade. First used by infantrymen on the battlefield and later favoured in a shortened staff version by the wives of the Samurai warriors.

Ninja

Collective term for the three levels of *genin*, *chunin* and *jonin*. Also known as shinobi. One who practises the art of ninjutsu.

Ninja-to (or ninja-ken)

Ninja sword. Its straight-edged blade was much shorter than that employed by the Samurai.

Glossary

Ninpo

Higher order of ninjutsu in the esoteric evolutionary scale.

Nunchaku

Two wooden batons linked together by a short chain or cord. This is a truly awesome weapon and can be successfully used to defend against sword strikes, in close combat against more than one person, strangulation and wrist locks. Used originally as a rice flail, like the Kama it can be found throughout Asia. In the hands of the ninja it has been said that the nunchaku looked as though it has a life of its own.

Obi

The wide sash-like belt worn by the Samurai in which they kept numerous personal effects. The ninja's obi was full of various objects to aid him on his mission. Again, given the ninja's versatility the obi could be used to bind a prisoner or even effect an escape by using it as rope.

Oda Nobunaga

Japanese Shogun who was the avowed enemy of all ninja. His troops lost the battle of Tensho Iga no Ran in 1579 against the massed ninja clans.

Glossary

Omyodo

Ancient science, thought to be of Chinese origin, which includes the arts of divination and astrology.

Onshin jutsu

Ninja art of invisibility, or the art of making oneself invisible by blending or melting into the available background. Methods of camouflage used by the ninja in order to observe without being seen. Use of various coloured uniforms by the ninja helped the ninja become invisible at will.

Ronin

The ronin were masterless Samurai who roamed the country like mercenaries, usually for hire and would work for anyone who would hire them. However, after Japan opened up its doors to the outside world many ronin took jobs as security enforcers or police-men.

Russia

With the aid of ninja espionage agents and covert operators Japan was able to glean much information about Russian troop and shipping movements in its preparation for the Russo-Sino War of 1904-05. Their victory over Russia was heralded around the world as a great triumph for the tiny emergent nation of Japan. The war concluded by the Treaty of Portsmouth in 1905 saw Port Arthur and half of the island of Sakhalin ceded to Japan.

Ryu

Japanese word for school or style.

Samin-jutsu

Ninja art of hypnotism.

Samurai

'One who serves'. The knightly warriors of feudal Japan.

Sekigahara

The last great battle fought by the Samurai of medieval Japan in AD1600. The defeat of Ishida Mitsunari in this bloodiest of battles left the way open for the Tokugawa shogunate to rule all the country for the next 250 years. Today it is a much visited tourist site.

Glossary

Sensei

The Japanese term for teacher or instructor. A ninja blackbelt would be addressed as sensei. This term has carried over to the West and it is used instead of Mr.

Shadows of Iga

Ninja appreciation and training society founded by American ninja practitioner Stephen Hayes, who among others has been the main force behind the growth and interest of ninjutsu in the West.

Shinobi

Original name by which the ninja were known.

Shinobikatana

Literally translated as the stealers-in sword, this was the ninja's sword.

Shinobishozuki

Ninja uniform. The ninja outfit was usually reversible and had many concealed pockets.

Shinobi-zue

Ninja staff which held a length of chain inside with a heavy weighted end.

Glossary

Shinto

Indigenous animistic religion of Japan. The word means 'divine spirit way' and is based upon ancestor worship among other things.

Shogun

Japanese military dictator who ruled the country with an iron fist and operated from his own head-quarters known as the Bakufu rather than from the Emperor's castle. Realistically for most of Japan's history the Emperor has mostly been a puppet figure head rather than having any real power.

Shorinji-Kempo

A Japanese martial art similar to karate with a blending of jujitsu principles. It was founded by Doshin-So, who was the style's first headmaster. Following his death the organization is now headed by his daughter. The logo for the style is the ancient Sanskrit symbol of the reversed swastika .

Shuko

Metal band that slipped over the hand, concealing four sharp spikes on the palm side. They were used in pairs for scaling castle walls and other difficult heights. Used as a defence and attack weapon against

Glossary

the sword, the metal spikes would rake the face of an attacker.

Shuriken

Multi-pointed throwing stars used as weapons by ninja agents. These stars, which came in all shapes and sizes, often had the ends tipped in poison. They were carried concealed in a ninja's uniform. Also known as *shaken*.

Sojutsu

Ninja spear art.

Sun Tsu

Chinese military genius who wrote a treatise on warfare called *Art of War*. The ninja clans are said to have arisen from the teachings of this book. Even today it is widely read.

Tabi

Ninja split-toed shoe or heavy sock.

Glossary

Taijutsu

Grappling or body art of ninjutsu. All ninjutsu practised today consists of 90 per cent taijutsu and is the
mainstay of the style.

Tanto

Short dirk or dagger of Japanese weaponry.

Tekagi

Similar to the *shuko* but only worn on the legs. Used
in pairs this instrument was useful as an aid for climbing walls and trees.

Tetsubishi *see* Caltrops

Tofu

Soft beancurd made from soya beans. Standard ration
for the field ninja when out on a mission.

Tokugawa Ieyasu

Founder of the Tokugawa shogunate in 1603. His
family ruled Japan for 250 years.

Glossary

Tsuba

Hand guard of a sword. The ninja's tsuba was square shaped rather than the customary round or oval shape of the Samurai weapon.

Yamabushi

Mountain warrior hermit priests.

Yari

Spear of the Japanese footsoldier.

Yoko Aruki

Special ninja method of walking for stealth. The word means 'sideways walking'.

Yumi

A short bow very different from the one used in Kyudo. The ninja were excellent archers and highly accurate. Quite often the arrow would be tipped with a poisonous substance so that even a slight wound would infect the Samurai and death would almost always follow.

Glossary

Zanshin

A state of mind cultivated in many Japanese martial arts. The practitioner is calm and aware of his opponent's every movement. The Samurai cultivated the art of *zanshin* to quite epic proportions. And it was this practice that kept them at peak performance when they were not involved in battles.

Zen

Religious philosophy that claims one can reach satori (enlightenment) through strict meditational practices. It was very much part and parcel of the Samurai's daily existence.

Index

Index

Index

Index

Index

Index

Index

Index

Index